Operations Research for Social Good:

A Practitioner's Introduction Using SAS® and Python

Natalia Summerville
Rob Pratt

sas.com/books

The correct bibliographic citation for this manual is as follows: Summerville, Natalia and Rob Pratt. 2023. *Operations Research for Social Good: A Practitioner's Introduction Using SAS® and Python.* Cary, NC: SAS Institute Inc.

Operations Research for Social Good: A Practitioner's Introduction Using SAS® and Python

ISBN 978-1-68580-005-5 (Hardcover)
ISBN 978-1-955977-83-8 (Paperback)
ISBN 978-1-955977-84-5 (Web PDF)
ISBN 978-1-955977-85-2 (EPUB)
ISBN 978-1-68580-004-8 (Kindle)

SAS Institute Inc., SAS Campus Drive, Cary, NC 27513-2414

October 2023

Operations Research for Social Good:
A Practitioner's Introduction
Using SAS and Python

Natalia Summerville and Rob Pratt

Contents

About this Book

What Does This Book Cover?

This book's purpose is to showcase Operations Research (OR) methodologies to applications targeted to make this world a better place. This book also provides skills and practical examples to model and solve OR problems with both SAS and Python.

Each use case is a real-life application that has been implemented and proven successful. We solve use cases with both SAS and Python, driving students to learn both programming languages to solve OR problems and giving professors flexibility to choose which technology to focus on in their classes.

This book does not cover operations research theory or optimization algorithms. Instead, it focuses on problem modeling and formulation.

Is This Book for You?

This book is for data scientists, analytics and operations research practitioners, and graduate-level students interested in learning optimization modeling with applied use cases.

What Are the Prerequisites for This Book?

Knowledge of linear algebra (specifically algebraic summation syntax) is needed.

What Should You Know about the Examples?

All examples in the book are formulated with SAS and Python, providing helpful coding syntax to the readers. All applications are based on real-life Data4Good projects.

Software Used to Develop the Book's Content

SAS OPTMODEL and Python/Pyomo.

Example Code and Data

You can access the example code and data for this book by linking to its author page at https://support.sas.com/authors.

SAS OnDemand for Academics

This book is compatible with SAS OnDemand for Academics. If you are using SAS OnDemand for Academics, then begin here: https://www.sas.com/en_us/software/on-demand-for-academics.html.

Where Are the Exercise Solutions?

Selected problem solutions can be found at the end of the book.

We Want to Hear from You

SAS Press books are written by SAS Users for SAS Users. We welcome your participation in their development and your feedback on SAS Press books that you are using. Please visit sas.com/books to do the following:

- Sign up to review a book
- Recommend a topic

- Request information on how to become a SAS Press author
- Provide feedback on a book

Learn more about these authors by visiting their author pages, where you can download free book excerpts, access example code and data, read the latest reviews, get updates, and more:

- https://support.sas.com/summerville
- https://support.sas.com/pratt

About the Authors

Natalia Summerville is the Director of Applied Data Science in the Strategy and Innovation Division at Memorial Sloan Kettering Cancer Center. Her team develops data analytics products to support hospital strategy and innovations in care delivery as well as cutting-edge cancer research. Previously, she led a team of Operations Research and Machine Learning experts at SAS, building analytical engines for customers across industries such as Health Care, Life Sciences, Retail, and Manufacturing. Natalia has been teaching undergrad and grad-level classes in Operations Research, Data Analytics, and Machine Learning since 2005, and she is currently an Adjunct Professor at Duke University. She is deeply passionate about the Data4Good movement and has been collaborating with many non-profit and mission-driven organizations to implement data analytics for social good. She is a board member within the "Pro-Bono Analytics" committee and is part of the "Franz Edelman Award" committee at INFORMS.

Rob Pratt has worked at SAS since 2000 and is a Senior Manager in the Scientific Computing Department in the Analytics R&D Division. He manages a team of developers responsible for the optimization modeling language and solvers for linear, mixed integer linear, quadratic, and conic optimization. He earned a B.S. in Mathematics (with a second major in English) from the University of Dayton and both an M.S. in Mathematics and a Ph.D. in Operations Research from The University of North Carolina at Chapel Hill.

Learn more about these authors by visiting their author pages, where you can download free book excerpts, access example code and data, read the latest reviews, get updates, and more:
http://support.sas.com/summerville
http://support.sas.com/pratt

Dedication

To the bright memory of our dear, bubbly Naba. You will live forever in our hearts.

Chapter 1

Introduction: Mathematical Optimization and the Data4Good Movement

Data4Good is a broad initiative, encompassing many types of analytics implementations for nonprofit organizations and/or organizations with missions that focus on the greater good. Examples of Data4Good projects include humanitarian logistics supporting disaster relief, cancer treatment innovation, equitable access to children's playgrounds, and deforestation forecasting, among many others. Typically, these implementations are performed by data scientists and analytics professionals on a pro bono/volunteer basis due to limited budgets available for analytics within these organizations. Over the last decade, the Data4Good movement has been significantly expanding, motivating more and more analytics professionals to bring their skills to support mission-driven organizations.

However, most of these applications focus on descriptive/diagnostic analytics, sometimes on predictive analytics, and rarely on prescriptive analytics. Traditionally, only analytically mature organizations built end-to-end prescriptive analytics engines that included optimization models. This is mostly due to the specific (and scarce) mathematical expertise required to properly formulate optimization models that often need PhD-level skills, available data to support these formulations, and established processes to incorporate new decision-making support systems that focus on user adoption and end value. Despite the reduced number of optimization projects in Data4Good (as opposed to descriptive and predictive modeling projects), we are firm believers that optimization tools can be key to help these mission-driven organizations make better decisions and be more efficient in using their very limited resources.

In this book, we introduce optimization modeling concepts that can help any organization be more efficient but with Data4Good applications. All applications discussed in this book come from proven real-life implementations, albeit often simplified for teaching purposes.

We hope that by studying this book, you will not only familiarize yourself with optimization modeling and scripting (in both SAS and Python) but also learn heartwarming applications where optimization can make this world a better place.

Chapter 2

Mathematical Optimization Landscape

Mathematical optimization provides organizations with actionable insights and results that are fundamentally geared toward improving organizational efficiency. This value-driven focus places optimization on top of Prescriptive Analytics, a field that generates the highest competitive advantage to those organizations who decide to use their data to build and implement optimization tools. But before we dive into definitions and specific characteristics of mathematical optimization, let's review the three main Advanced Analytics areas and how they relate to each other.

2.1   Areas of Advanced Analytics

Advanced Analytics is typically classified into three (or four, depending on the source) categories based on their usage and competitive advantage for the organization. These areas are Descriptive/Diagnostic (some authors split these two into separate categories), Predictive, and Prescriptive, as shown in Figure 2.1.

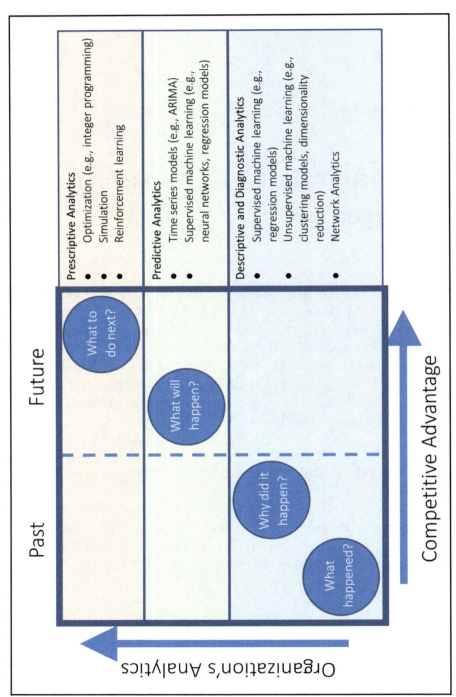

Figure 2.1: Areas of Advanced Analytics

Descriptive/Diagnostic Analytics

Descriptive and/or Diagnostic Analytics focuses on using data analysis to understand what has happened and why it has happened. Besides basic data analysis techniques such as scatter plots and correlation analysis, the most used Advanced Analytics models include:

- Clustering (Unsupervised Machine Learning) to understand groups of observations and their similarities
- Network Analytics to describe patterns in interconnected data
- Regression Analysis (Supervised Machine Learning) to understand causal relationships

For example, we might want to understand the differences between groups of patients based on their molecular characteristics from lab tests using clustering techniques. We might also be interested in identifying the most relevant production settings that influence key quality metrics in wallboard manufacturing using regression models.

Predictive Analytics

Predictive Analytics uses statistical analysis to forecast future states. Besides naïve forecasting techniques such as year-over-year and moving averages, some typical forecasting models are:

- ARIMA models (Time Series Forecasting) to derive historical patterns from past sequential data and predict future observations by using those historical patterns
- Recurrent Neural Networks (Supervised Machine Learning) to predict future states based on previous states and their interactions

For example, time series models would forecast weekly product sales for a specific grocery store or expected daily arrivals for labor and delivery unit in a hospital.

Prescriptive Analytics

Prescriptive Analytics focuses on providing the best possible future action to achieve organizational goals. Besides techniques such as heuristic rule-based approaches and decision analysis, the most typically used Advanced Analytics tools are:

- Optimization, which includes an algebraic representation of the business problem, including relevant goals, key performance indicators (KPIs), rules, and limitations, as well as mathematical algorithms that find the best possible decisions that satisfy those rules while maximizing or minimizing those KPIs
- Simulation models to build a digital system representation, including stochastic distributions of relevant parameters, and to run what-if analysis and evaluate decision options
- Markov Chains that model systems where there are transitions between states according to probabilistic rules

For example, we might need to find the best possible schedule for retail employees, aiming to cover shifts with highest demand while minimizing overtime using mathematical optimization.

The three Advanced Analytics areas are closely related, and typically all of them are required for a successful analytical implementation. For example, very often within optimization models we need to incorporate forecasted demand for a product, or relationships between manufacturing settings and relevant KPIs, which in turn use time series and regression models, respectively.

2.2   Process to Produce an Optimal Solution

To generate an optimal solution via mathematical optimization, four main steps need to happen after thorough data exploration, validation, and predictive model building (if required). These steps are highlighted in Figure 2.2.

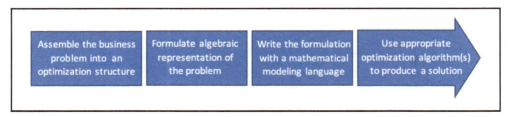

Figure 2.2: Optimization Process

We first need to assemble the problem into an optimization structure, which includes identifying the following components (also presented in Table 2.1):

Table 2.1: Optimization Components		
Optimization Component	Definition	Examples
Decision Variables	Controllable actions	Promotion discounts Selection of investment funds Classroom assignment to student groups
Constraints	Rules and limitations	Do not let profit be negative Stay within available budget Each group needs to have a classroom
Objective Function(s)	Goals for key performance indicators	Maximize revenue Minimize final inventory Maximize classroom utilization

- Decision variables are the controllable actions that users can take. For example, a pricing analyst decides how much price promotion discount to allocate to certain products and when.
- Constraints are all the rules and limitations that restrict those decisions. For example, the promotion discounts must not lead to a negative profit across all products.
- Objective functions are specific goals for the KPIs that the organization wants to achieve in this decision-making process. For example, the user might want to maximize revenue.

It is typically helpful to have those components written in a natural language before moving to the next step. For example:

- I need to decide how to price my products (decision variables).
- I want to achieve highest revenue (objective function).
- Margin cannot be negative (constraint).
- Demand for each product is expected to be $100 - 0.2 * Price$ (constraint).

Please notice that the demand equation above (albeit simplified for this example) requires a predictive model that explains the relationship between price and demand.

Once there is clear understanding of the components described above, we need to formulate this problem mathematically, using appropriate algebra. For example:

$$\text{maximize} \quad \sum_p Demand_p \times Price_p$$

$$\text{subject to} \quad \sum_p (Price_p - Cost_p) \geq 0$$

$$Demand_p = 100 - 0.2 Price_p \quad \text{for all } p \in \text{PRODUCTS}$$

$$Price_p \geq 0 \quad \text{for all } p \in \text{PRODUCTS}$$

The next step is expressing the algebraic formulation in a mathematical programming language like SAS OPTMODEL or Python Pyomo that use an intuitive coding syntax to facilitate an easy translation between the math and the code.

The final step is to call an efficient algorithm (sometimes called a solver) to produce an optimal solution. In the example above, the algorithm would return an optimum price for each product that would generate the maximum revenue while making sure profit is nonnegative.

2.3 Types of Optimization Models

Optimization models are classified based on the mathematical characteristics of the algebraic representation of the problem such as linearity in constraints/objective functions and types of decision variables used. Some of the most used optimization models include Linear Programming (LP), Integer Programming (IP), Mixed Integer Linear Programming (MILP), Nonlinear Programming (NLP), and Multicriteria Optimization. This list is not exhaustive. Differences among these types of models are shown in Table 2.2.

Table 2.2: Most Used Types of Optimization				
Optimization Component	Linear Programming	Mixed Integer Linear Programming	Nonlinear Programming	Multicriteria Optimization
Decision Variables	Continuous	Continuous, Integer, or Binary	Continuous	Continuous, Integer, or Binary
Constraints	Linear	Linear	Nonlinear	Linear or Nonlinear
Objective Function(s)	One	One	One	More than one

Network optimization models deserve special mention. Many well-studied formulations such as Shortest Path or Traveling Salesman have MILP models. However, their specific structural characteristics enable specialized algorithms to generate solutions much faster than a typical MILP algorithm such as Branch-and-Bound would. Therefore, it is often desirable, when appropriate, to reformulate MILP models as Network models to take advantage of their specific structure and specialized algorithms.

2.4   Optimality and Algorithmic Performance

Some optimization problems can be very complex (in terms of number of decision variables, number of constraints, nonlinearity, and integrality of variables, among others). This complexity translates into potentially long running times for the solution algorithms and sometimes inability to achieve an optimal solution. However, in practice, many times even if a feasible solution is not globally optimal, it can still provide significant business value over the status quo.

2.5   Example Application – Medical Resource Optimization

In March 2020, the COVID-19 global pandemic forced hospitals to reassign most of their resources in order to maintain Emergency Rooms (ERs) and Intensive Care Units (ICUs) ready to support the population's growing need for emergency COVID-19 care and put on hold many of the elective surgeries and procedures that clinics and hospitals offered. SAS and Cleveland Clinic partnered to develop a mathematical model to support decision-making regarding reopening these optional services, considering the capacity limitations on manpower, equipment, and COVID-19 tests, among others.

This problem was formulated as a Multicriteria MILP mathematical model. The components of the model are described as follows.

Decision Variables

Controllable decision variables in this model were defined as the selection of subservices to reopen and the reopening dates.

Constraints

The reopening of subservices and number of patients accepted had to adhere to many constraints, the most significant of which are:

- The capacity of each resource at a facility, their services, and their corresponding subservices cannot be exceeded.
- The utilization of ICU resources at a facility cannot exceed a specified upper limit.
- The number of patients accepted at a facility will never exceed the maximum forecasted demand.
- The total number of daily emergency surgery and patients accepted across all facilities should not exceed the number of daily rapid tests available.
- If a subservice is open at a facility/service-line on a day, it should remain open for the remainder of the horizon (logical condition).

Objective Functions

This model had two objective functions to reboot clinics' cash flow, which in turn enables further support for emergency care:

- Maximize the total revenue
- Maximize the total margin

Revenue and margin are functions of the number of patients accepted over the planning horizon.

More detailed information, as well as the full code, can be found at https://github.com/sassoftware/medical-resource-optimization.

Many other very useful optimization model examples and their SAS code can be found at https://support.sas.com/rnd/app/examples/ORexamples.html#MPE.

Chapter 3

Use Case Structure and Code Initialization

We will now describe the structure of each chapter and use case as well as the required code initialization to be able to run the code provided in this book. This is relevant for a smooth progression through the use cases and their associated sections.

3.1 Use Case Structure

Each chapter first describes a type of mathematical optimization model at a high level, pointing to relevant bibliography in case the reader would like to learn more of the theory behind the models and algorithms. Then the concepts are discussed further through use cases, typically with increasing complexity. Each use case is structured in the following way.

3.1.1 Introduction

The introduction section of each use case has a high-level overview of the optimization application and its real-world impact. All use cases in this book come from real-life applications, with some modifications to make the formulation appropriate to introduce optimization modeling to the reader. This section also gives due credit to original authors and provides links where the reader can find more information on the original application.

3.1.2   Problem Definition

This section formalizes the description of the application with optimization elements: goals/objective functions, rules/constraints, and controls/decision variables.

3.1.3   Data and Settings Inputs

We loosely differentiate between two types of inputs: data and settings (even though both can be ingested from data tables).

- *Data inputs* are defined here as inputs that are typically provided from databases and can be quite large, for example, cost of each food element, product demand, and so on.
- *Settings inputs* are defined as single data points the application user can modify to shape the problem further, for example, overall budget, maximum number of products to include in price promotion, and so on.

A detailed data dictionary is provided for each use case that includes all data tables to be read within the code. The data dictionary contains the names of the data tables, the variables, their types, and a description of each variable. Finally, we include a small snapshot (typically just a couple records) of each table to give further insight into the data structure. Please notice any modifications to the data structure would require code modification as well.

All use case data are provided in the companion materials for this book as CSV files.

3.1.4   Mathematical Formulation

Before defining the equations for the constraints and objective function(s) for the use case, we introduce all nomenclature and its detailed descriptions, including dimensions (or sets), data parameters (from input data), user settings (either hard-coded or read from input settings tables), and decision variables.

Then we mathematically formulate all constraints (using the nomenclature as detailed before) and describe each constraint. Finally, we mathematically formulate and describe the objective function(s).

3.1.5 Mathematical Formulation and SAS Model

In this section, we present the SAS OPTMODEL code required to formulate the use case. For the reader's convenience, we match each piece of the
code with the associated mathematical formulation to promote code syntax
intuition in the reader. An example is shown in Table 3.1.

MATHEMATICS	SAS CODE
$t \in \text{TIMES}$	`set TIMES;`
capacity	`num capacity = 40;`
$NumStart_t$	`var NumStart {TIMES} >= 0 integer;`
$\sum_t NumStart_t \leq capacity$	`con CapacityCon:` `  sum {t in TIMES} NumStart[t] <= capacity;`

Table 3.1: SAS Code Example

3.1.6 SAS Output

This section shares a screenshot of the summary output provided by SAS
OPTMODEL after running the code. An example is provided in Figure 3.1.
This output contains some relevant information such as the name of the solver
and algorithm used, the solution status (optimal, infeasible, etc.), the optimum
value of the objective function (if found), and more information related to the
algorithmic progression. Any extra values that we requested to be printed will
appear as well.

3.1.7 Mathematical Formulation and Python Model

Similarly to the SAS OPTMODEL section, here we provide detailed syntax
using Python's Pyomo package and associate this syntax with each piece of
the mathematical formulation. An example is shown in Table 3.2.

The SAS System

The SAS System

The OPTMODEL Procedure

Solution Summary	
Solver	MILP
Algorithm	Branch and Cut
Objective Function	MinTotalShortage
Solution Status	Optimal
Objective Value	46
Relative Gap	0
Absolute Gap	0
Primal Infeasibility	0
Bound Infeasibility	0
Integer Infeasibility	0
Best Bound	46
Nodes	1
Solutions Found	6
Iterations	39
Presolve Time	0.00
Solution Time	0.01

MinTotalShortage	MinMaxShortage
46	8

Figure 3.1: SAS Output

Table 3.2: Python Code Example

MATHEMATICS	PYTHON CODE
$capacity$	`m.capacity = Param()`
$t \in \text{TIMES}$	`m.times = Set()`
$NumStart_t$	`m.NumStart = Var(m.times, domain=NonNegativeIntegers)`

$\sum_t NumStart_t \leq capacity$	`def Capacity_Rule(m):`
	` return (sum(m.NumStart[t] for t in m.times) <= m.capacity)`
	`m.Capacity = Constraint(rule=Capacity_Rule)`

3.1.8   Python Output

This section shares a screenshot of the summary output provided by Pyomo after running the code. An example is provided in Figure 3.2. This output contains some relevant information such as the status, the termination condition, some statistics on algorithmic progression, and any extra values that we requested to be printed.

```
- Status: ok
  Termination condition: optimal
  Statistics:
    Branch and bound:
      Number of bounded subproblems: 1
      Number of created subproblems: 1
  Error rc: 0
  Time: 0.042832136154174805

Optimum Total Shortage Value:
46.0
Max Shortage Value:
7.0
```

Figure 3.2: Python Output

3.1.9   Output Results

Finally, we provide a snapshot (a couple records) of the output results generated by the code and explain their interpretation. These results refer specifically to the optimum values of the decision variables.

3.2   Code Initialization

It is common in optimization applications to use two types of software: a modeling language that algebraically expresses the mathematical model and a solver that solves the problem. This book's focus is the art of modeling optimization applications, so we strongly rely on the modeling language software, specifically OPTMODEL for SAS and Pyomo for Python. We then make calls to the appropriate solvers to produce a solution. This is the typical pipeline followed by optimization practitioners, unless the size of the problem exceeds the capacity of the existing solvers and the user needs to design specific algorithms (sometimes heuristics) to generate solutions for the problem.

To be able to run the mathematical formulation code shown in the use cases' SAS/Python sections, we encourage the reader to open the accompanying .sas and .ipynb files. Those files contain relevant setup lines of code such as:

- Importing CSV files into the appropriate form: SAS data set or pandas DataFrame
- Calling the appropriate procedure/packages
- Reading the SAS data set or pandas DataFrame into defined optimization parameters

These three steps are not detailed in the use case sections, and the reader needs to obtain the right syntax imported directly from the code files.

We will now describe the required installations for each software.

3.2.1   SAS Code Initialization

This book uses SAS Optimization in SAS Viya and the following relevant products:

- Modeling language: OPTMODEL
- Solvers: LP, MILP, NLP, network
- Code editor: SAS Studio

Detailed documentation is provided in [SAS23]. We strongly encourage readers to refer to this documentation when needed to better understand syntax and/or when code debugging is necessary.

At the time of this book publication, SAS provides two free trial options, and the code provided in this book can be run in any of these:

- SAS Viya for Learners.
  https://www.sas.com/en_us/software/viya-for-learners.html
  The reader needs to have an academic email to be able to request access. This version contains the latest SAS platform called SAS Viya and includes SAS OPTMODEL. Depending on your academic institution, personal data uploads might not be allowed.

- SAS OnDemand for Academics
  https://support.sas.com/en/software/ondemand-for-academics-support.html
  The reader does not need to have a specific type of email to request access. This trial is built on the SAS 9 platform and might have more limited features than SAS Viya. The only data limitations in this option are size-related.

It is also relevant to mention that SAS does offer an alternative formulation language (sasoptpy) that supports writing the model in Python while calling SAS solvers. Documentation can be found here: https://sassoftware.github.io/sasoptpy

3.2.2 Python Code Initialization

This book uses Python 3.10.4 [dt22f] and the following packages:

- Modeling language: Pyomo 6.4.2.
  Software documentation can be found in [dt22e] and accompanying research in [BHH+21] and [HWW11].
- Solvers: GLPK version 5.0 and IPOPT version 3.14.9.
  Software documentation can be found in [dt12] and [dt22a] and accompanying research in [WB06].
- Code editor: Jupyter Notebook 6.4.12.
  Documentation can be found in [dt22b].
- Support: pandas 1.4.3 and NumPy 1.23.3.
  Documentation can be found in [dt22d] and [dt22c] and accompanying research in [dt20], [WM10], and [HMvdW+20].

Chapter 4

Linear Programming

Linear Programming (LP) is a fundamental optimization methodology and forms the basis of several other areas in Operations Research. This chapter first reviews LP concepts and then presents two use cases based on real applications, followed by practice problems related to these use cases.

4.1 Concepts Review

A *Linear Programming (LP) problem* is an optimization problem with all variables continuous, a linear objective function, and all constraints linear. In mathematical notation, the problem is to maximize or minimize a linear function $\sum_{j=1}^{n} c_j x_j$ subject to linear constraints $\sum_{j=1}^{n} a_{i,j} x_j = b_i$ for $i \in \{1, \ldots, m\}$ and $\ell_j \leq x_j \leq u_j$ for $j \in \{1, \ldots, n\}$. Here, the c_j values are called *objective coefficients*, the $a_{i,j}$ values are called *constraint coefficients*, b_i is the *right-hand side*, and ℓ_j and u_j are *lower and upper bounds*, respectively, for the decision variable x_j. Commonly, the decision variables represent physical quantities for which $\ell_j = 0$ and $u_j = \infty$, but either bound can be finite or infinite. Because everything is linear, an LP problem can alternatively be represented in matrix-vector form as follows: maximize or minimize $c^\top x$ subject to $Ax = b$ and $\ell \leq x \leq u$. For simplicity, the notation used here expresses each constraint as an equality, but most LP solvers accept any combination of $=$, $\leq$, and $\geq$ constraints.

To solve an LP problem, several alternative algorithms are common:

- The *primal simplex method*, devised by George Dantzig in 1947, proceeds in two phases. The first phase ("Phase I") finds a *feasible* solution that satisfies all constraints, and the second phase ("Phase II") improves the feasible solution to an *optimal* solution that both satisfies all constraints and optimizes the objective function. This algorithm is especially useful when you want to solve a sequence of LPs in which every feasible solution of one LP is feasible to the subsequent LP, as often happens when new decision variables are added to an existing problem. A *warm start* procedure can exploit this structure to skip Phase I instead of starting from scratch.

- The *sifting algorithm* is a column-generation variant of the primal simplex method that considers only a small subset of the variables at a time and introduces others as needed based on reduced costs. This algorithm tends to perform better when the number of variables is much larger than the number of constraints.

- The *dual simplex method* similarly proceeds in two phases but is more efficient for warm starting when new constraints are added to a problem, as happens during the branch-and-bound algorithm for mixed integer linear programming, to be discussed in Chapter 5.

- The *network simplex algorithm* is efficient for problems that consist mostly of a network structure, such as in the minimum-cost network flow problem.

- The *interior point algorithm* can be efficient for large LPs with millions of decision variables, in part because it can naturally use parallel processing.

- *Dantzig-Wolfe decomposition* can perform well for problems where the constraint matrix has block-angular structure, that is, where the problem decomposes into multiple subproblems that are linked together by only a small percentage of the overall number of constraints. For more information about the automated Dantzig-Wolfe implementation in SAS, see the decomposition algorithm chapter in [SAS23].

SAS provides all of these LP algorithms, and the default choice is based on the problem structure. A *concurrent* option can run multiple LP algorithms simultaneously on multiple threads, returning an optimal solution whenever the first algorithm finishes. For more information about the LP solver in SAS, see the linear programming solver chapter in [SAS23].

In Python, different linear programming solvers can be called, for example the open source solver GLPK [dt12].

For in-depth information about linear models and solution algorithms, please refer to [BT97].

4.2   Use Case: The Nutritious Supply Chain: A Food Basket Optimization

The United Nations World Food Programme (WFP) is the largest humanitarian agency fighting hunger worldwide, reaching around 80 million people with food assistance in 75 countries each year. A comprehensive model was developed by Peters et al. [PSG$^+$21] to support WFP by simultaneously optimizing the food basket, sourcing plan, and routing plan of a recovery operation. In this section, we will focus on a simplified food basket optimization, addressed in the comprehensive research mentioned above. This research won the 2021 Franz Edelman Award for Achievement in Advanced Analytics, Operations Research, and Management Science from INFORMS.

4.2.1   Problem Definition

The food basket optimization problem focuses on finding the optimum food commodities to be included in the package, such that required nutrition levels are achieved at minimum cost.

4.2.2   Data and Settings Inputs

This application requires data on the nutrient levels for each food commodity to be considered (data input), as well as the cost per commodity (data input) and the minimum required level for each nutrient (data input).

The data dictionary in Table 4.1 contains more detailed information about the tables and the variables.

Table 4.1: Data Dictionary			
Data Table	Variable Name	Variable Type	Variable Description
INPUT_FOOD	Food	Char	Name of the food commodity (e.g., Eggs_Raw)
INPUT_FOOD	Cost	Num	Cost of the food commodity per ration (e.g., 3.5)
INPUT_FOOD_NUTR	Food	Char	Name of the food commodity (e.g., Eggs_Raw)
INPUT_FOOD_NUTR	Nutr	Char	Name of the nutrient (e.g., Fiber)
INPUT_FOOD_NUTR	Value	Num	Amount of the nutrient in the food commodity ration (e.g., 42)
INPUT_MIN_INTAKE	Nutr	Char	Name of the nutrient (e.g., Fiber)
INPUT_MIN_INTAKE	Req	Num	Minimum amount of nutrient required in a healthy diet (e.g., 1800)

Tables 4.2, 4.3, and 4.4 show snapshots of the input data.

Table 4.2: INPUT_FOOD Data Snapshot

Food	Cost
Beef	6
Cheese	0.5
Corn Meal	0.5

Table 4.3: INPUT_FOOD_NUTR Data Snapshot

Food	Nutr	Value
Corn Meal	Calories	360
Corn Meal	Protein	9
Corn Meal	Fiber	1

Table 4.4: INPUT_MIN_INTAKE Data Snapshot

Nutr	Req
Calories	1800
Protein	45
Fiber	26

4.2.3 Mathematical Formulation

Dimensions

The dimensions relevant in this use case are the sets of food commodities and nutrients, as shown in Table 4.5.

Table 4.5: Dimensions	
Dimension Name	Dimension Description
$f \in$ FOOD	Set of food commodities
$n \in$ NUTR	Set of nutrients

Data Parameters

Table 4.6 shows the input parameters read from the INPUT_FOOD, INPUT_FOOD_NUTR, and INPUT_MIN_INTAKE tables.

Table 4.6: Data Parameters	
Parameter Name	Parameter Description
$foodCost_f$	Cost of food commodity f
$nutrVal_{n,f}$	Amount of nutrient n in food commodity f
$nutrReq_n$	Minimum requirement for nutrient n

Decision Variables

The key decision variable is the amount of food commodity to include in the food basket, as shown in Table 4.7.

Table 4.7: Decision Variables	
Variable Name	Variable Description
$FoodAmt_f$	Amount of food commodity f to include in the food basket

Constraints

This use case imposes the following constraints:

$$\sum_f nutrVal_{n,f} \times FoodAmt_f \geq nutrReq_n \qquad\qquad \text{for all } n \qquad (4.1)$$

Constraint (4.1) assures required levels of all nutrients are achieved with the food basket.

Objective Function

The objective in this use case is to minimize the total cost of the food basket:

$$\min\ TotalCost = \sum_f foodCost_f \times FoodAmt_f$$

4.2.4   Mathematical Formulation and SAS Model

Tables 4.8 and 4.9 show the mathematical formulation and the corresponding SAS code. The full code can be found in the supporting materials.

Table 4.8: SAS Code for Sets, Parameters, and Variables	
MATHEMATICS	SAS CODE
$f \in \text{FOOD}$	`set <str> FOOD;`
$n \in \text{NUTR}$	`set <str> NUTR;`
$foodCost_f$	`num foodCost {FOOD};`
$nutrReq_n$	`num nutrReq {NUTR};`
$nutrVal_{n,f}$	`num nutrVal {NUTR, FOOD};`
$FoodAmt_f$	`var FoodAmt {FOOD} >= 0;`

Table 4.9: SAS Code for Constraints and Objective Function

$\sum_f nutrVal_{n,f} \times FoodAmt_f \geq$ $nutrReq_n$ for all n	```con Nutrition {n in NUTR}: sum {f in FOOD} nutrVal[n,f] * FoodAmt[f] >= nutrReq[n];```
min $TotalCost =$ $\sum_f foodCost_f \times FoodAmt_f$	```min TotalCost = sum {f in FOOD} foodCost[f] * FoodAmt[f];```

4.2.5 SAS Output

Figure 4.1 shows the Solution Summary produced by the SAS code, including the optimum value for the objective function.

The SAS System

The OPTMODEL Procedure

Solution Summary	
Solver	LP
Algorithm	Dual Simplex
Objective Function	TotalCost
Solution Status	Optimal
Objective Value	3.9672110553
Primal Infeasibility	0
Dual Infeasibility	0
Bound Infeasibility	0
Iterations	4
Presolve Time	0.00
Solution Time	0.00

Figure 4.1: SAS Output

4.2.6   Mathematical Formulation and Python Model

Tables 4.10 and 4.11 show the mathematical formulation and the corresponding Python code. The full code can be found in the supporting materials.

Table 4.10: Python Code for Sets, Parameters, and Variables

MATHEMATICS	PYTHON CODE
$f \in$ FOOD	`m.food = Set()`
$n \in$ NUTR	`m.nutr = Set()`
$foodCost_f$	`m.foodCost = Param(m.food)`
$nutrReq_n$	`m.nutrReq = Param(m.nutr)`
$nutrVal_{n,f}$	`m.nutrVal = Param(m.nutr,m.food)`
$FoodAmt_f$	`m.FoodAmt = Var(m.food, domain=NonNegativeReals)`

Table 4.11: Python Code for Constraints and Objective Function

$\sum_f nutrVal_{n,f} \times FoodAmt_f \geq$ $nutrReq_n$ for all n	```def Nutr_Rule(m,n):```
	`  return (sum(m.nutrVal[n,f]*m.FoodAmt[f]`
	`  for f in m.food) >= m.nutrReq[n])`
	`m.Nutr = Constraint(m.nutr,rule=Nutr_Rule)`

min $TotalCost =$ $\sum_f foodCost_f \times FoodAmt_f$	```def Cost_Rule(m):```
	`  return (sum(m.foodCost[f]*m.FoodAmt[f]`
	`  for f in m.food))`
	`m.Cost = Objective(rule=Cost_Rule, sense=minimize)`

4.2.7   Python Output

Figure 4.2 shows the output produced by the Python code, including the optimum value for the objective function.

```
Solver Status:

- Status: ok
  Message: Ipopt 3.11.1\x3a Optimal Solution Found
  Termination condition: optimal
  Id: 0
  Error rc: 0
  Time: 0.040258169174194336

Optimum Objective Function Value:
3.9672110634577433
```

Figure 4.2: Python Output

4.2.8   Output Results

Table 4.12 shows a snapshot of the optimal results. This is the optimum amount (weight) for each food commodity to be included in the food basket.

Table 4.12: Optimal Results Data Snapshot

Food	Amt
Flour	0.93
Corn Meal	0
Oatmeal	5.87

4.3   Use Case: The Nutritious Supply Chain: Food Basket and Delivery Optimization

As mentioned in the previous use case, the United Nations World Food Programme (WFP) is the largest humanitarian agency fighting hunger worldwide, reaching around 80 million people with food assistance in 75 countries each year. In this section, we will expand the food basket optimization model to include optimum distribution decisions because different suppliers need to be considered.

4.3.1   Problem Definition

In addition to optimizing the food commodities to be included, we also determine the optimum suppliers for each food. Each food commodity can be shipped from different suppliers at different costs. Suppliers might also have different availability for each food commodity.

4.3.2   Data and Settings Inputs

This application requires data on the nutrient levels for each food commodity to be considered (data input) and the minimum required level for each nutrient (data input). We now also include supplier food commodity availability and cost (data input). In this use case, the availability and cost depend on the supplier.

The data dictionary in Table 4.13 contains more detailed information about the tables and the variables.

Table 4.13: Data Dictionary			
Data Table	Variable Name	Variable Type	Variable Description
INPUT_FOOD	Food	Char	Name of the food commodity (e.g., Eggs_Raw)
INPUT_FOOD	Cost	Num	Cost of the food commodity per ration (e.g., 3.5)
INPUT_FOOD_NUTR	Food	Char	Name of the food commodity (e.g., Eggs_Raw)
INPUT_FOOD_NUTR	Nutr	Char	Name of the nutrient (e.g., Fiber)
INPUT_FOOD_NUTR	Value	Num	Amount of the nutrient in the food commodity ration (e.g., 42)
INPUT_MIN_INTAKE	Nutr	Char	Name of the nutrient (e.g., Fiber)
INPUT_MIN_INTAKE	Req	Num	Minimum amount of nutrient required in a healthy diet (e.g., 1800)
INPUT_SUPPLIERS	Food	Char	Name of the food commodity (e.g., Eggs_Raw)
INPUT_SUPPLIERS	Supplier_ID	Num	Identification number of the supplier (e.g., 1)
INPUT_SUPPLIERS	Tcost	Char	Transportation cost of the food item provided by supplier (e.g., 2.5)
INPUT_SUPPLIERS	Avail	Char	Availability of the food item provided by supplier per measurement (e.g., 100)

Table 4.14 shows a snapshot of additional supplier input data, used together with Tables 4.2, 4.3, and 4.4.

Table 4.14: INPUT_SUPPLIERS Data Snapshot

Food	Supplier_ID	Tcost	Avail
Beef	1	0.1642	170
Beef	2	0.20	98
Beef	3	0.35	120

4.3.3 Mathematical Formulation

User-defined Settings

Table 4.15 shows an additional user-defined setting that is required in this formulation.

Table 4.15: User-defined Settings	
Setting Name	Setting Description
numBaskets	Total number of baskets that need to be shipped

Dimensions

The dimensions relevant in this use case are the sets of food commodities, nutrients, and suppliers, as shown in Table 4.16.

Table 4.16: Dimensions	
Dimension Name	Dimension Description
$f \in$ FOOD	Set of food commodities
$n \in$ NUTR	Set of nutrients
$s \in$ SUPP	Set of suppliers

Data Parameters

Table 4.17 shows the input parameters read from the INPUT_FOOD, INPUT_FOOD_NUTR, INPUT_MIN_INTAKE, and INPUT_SUPPLIERS tables.

Table 4.17: Data Parameters	
Parameter Name	Parameter Description
$foodCost_f$	Cost of food commodity, independent of supplier f
$foodTcost_{f,s}$	Transportation cost of food commodity f from supplier s
$foodAvail_{f,s}$	Availability of food commodity f from supplier s
$nutrReq_n$	Minimum requirement for nutrient n
$nutrVal_{n,f}$	Amount of nutrient n in food commodity f

Decision Variables

The key decision variable is the amount of each food commodity to ship from each supplier, as shown in Table 4.18.

Table 4.18: Decision Variables	
Variable Name	Variable Description
$FoodAmt_{f,s}$	Amount of commodity f to include in the food basket from supplier s

Constraints

This use case imposes the following constraints:

$$\sum_{f,s} nutrVal_{n,f} \times FoodAmt_{f,s} \geq numBaskets \times nutrReq_n \quad \text{for all } n \quad (4.2)$$

$$FoodAmt_{f,s} \leq foodAvail_{f,s} \quad \text{for all } f, s \quad (4.3)$$

Constraint (4.2) assures required levels of all nutrients are achieved for all the baskets to be shipped, and constraint (4.3) prohibits exceeding the given availability of food commodities.

Objective Function

The objective in this use case is to minimize the total cost of all food baskets, including transportation cost:

$$\min TotalCost = \sum_{f,s} (foodCost_f + foodTcost_{f,s}) FoodAmt_{f,s}$$

4.3.4 Mathematical Formulation and SAS Model

Tables 4.19 and 4.20 show the mathematical formulation and the corresponding SAS code. The full code can be found in the supporting materials.

Table 4.19: SAS Code for Sets, Parameters, and Variables	
MATHEMATICS	SAS CODE
$numBaskets$	`num numBaskets = 85;`
$f \in$ FOOD	`set <str> FOOD;`
$n \in$ NUTR	`set <str> NUTR;`
$s \in$ SUPP	`set SUPP;`
$foodCost_f$	`num foodCost {FOOD};`
$foodTcost_{f,s}$	`num foodTcost {FOOD, SUPP};`
$foodAvail_{f,s}$	`num foodAvail {FOOD, SUPP};`
$nutrReq_n$	`num nutrReq {NUTR};`
$nutrVal_{n,f}$	`num nutrVal {NUTR, FOOD};`
$FoodAmt_{f,s}$	`var FoodAmt {FOOD, SUPP} >= 0;`

Table 4.20: SAS Code for Constraints and Objective Function

$\sum_{f,s} nutrVal_{n,f} \times FoodAmt_{f,s} \geq$ $numBaskets \times nutrReq_n$ for all n	```con Nutrition {n in NUTR}:```
	 ```sum {f in FOOD, s in SUPP} nutrVal[n,f] * FoodAmt[f,s]```
	 ```>= numBaskets * nutrReq[n];```

$FoodAmt_{f,s} \leq foodAvail_{f,s}$ for all f,s	```con Supply {f in FOOD, s in SUPP}:``` ```FoodAmt[f,s] <= foodAvail[f,s];```

$\min TotalCost =$ $\sum_{f,s}(foodCost_f + foodTcost_{f,s})FoodAmt_{f,s}$	```min TotalCost =```
	 ```sum {f in FOOD, s in SUPP}```
	 ```(foodCost[f] + foodTcost[f,s]) * FoodAmt[f,s];```

4.3.5   SAS Output

Figure 4.3 shows the Solution Summary produced by the SAS code, including the optimum value for the objective function.

The SAS System

The OPTMODEL Procedure

Solution Summary	
Solver	LP
Algorithm	Dual Simplex
Objective Function	TotalCost
Solution Status	Optimal
Objective Value	1430.0324819
Primal Infeasibility	0
Dual Infeasibility	0
Bound Infeasibility	0
Iterations	2
Presolve Time	0.01
Solution Time	0.02

Figure 4.3: SAS Output

4.3.6   Mathematical Formulation and Python Model

Tables 4.21 and 4.22 show the mathematical formulation and the corresponding Python code. The full code can be found in the supporting materials.

Table 4.21: Python Code for Sets, Parameters, and Variables

MATHEMATICS	PYTHON CODE
$numBaskets$	`m.numBaskets = 85`
$f \in$ FOOD	`m.food = Set()`
$n \in$ NUTR	`m.nutr = Set()`
$s \in$ SUPP	`m.supp = Set()`
$foodCost_f$	`m.foodCost = Param(m.food)`
$foodTcost_{f,s}$	`m.foodTcost = Param(m.food,m.supp)`
$foodAvail_{f,s}$	`m.foodAvail = Param(m.food,m.supp)`
$nutrReq_n$	`m.nutrReq = Param(m.nutr)`
$nutrVal_{n,f}$	`m.nutrVal = Param(m.nutr,m.food)`
$FoodAmt_{f,s}$	`m.FoodAmt = Var(m.food, m.supp, domain=NonNegativeReals)`

4.3.7   Python Output

Figure 4.4 shows the output produced by the Python code, including the optimum value for the objective function.

4.3.8   Output Results

Table 4.23 shows a snapshot of optimal results. These are the optimum amounts (weight) of each food commodity to request from each supplier.

Table 4.22: Python Code for Constraints and Objective Function

$$\sum_{f,s} nutrVal_{n,f} \times FoodAmt_{f,s} \geq \\ numBaskets \times nutrReq_n \text{ for all } n$$	```def Nutr_Rule(m,n):```
	 ``` return (sum(m.nutrVal[n,f]*m.FoodAmt[f,s]```
	 ``` for f in m.food for s in m.supp) >= m.numBaskets*m.nutrReq[n])```
	 ```m.Nutr = Constraint(m.nutr,rule=Nutr_Rule)```

$$FoodAmt_{f,s} \leq foodAvail_{f,s} \text{ for all } f,s$$	```def Food_Avail_Rule(m,f,s):```
	 ``` return (m.FoodAmt[f,s] <= m.foodAvail[f,s])```
	 ```m.Food_Avail = Constraint(m.food,m.supp,rule=Food_Avail_Rule)```

$$\min TotalCost = \\ \sum_{f,s}(foodCost_f + foodTcost_{f,s}) FoodAmt_{f,s}$$	```def Min_Cost_Rule(m):```
	 ``` return (sum(m.foodTcost[f,s] + m.foodCost[f]*m.FoodAmt[f,s]```
	 ``` for f in m.food for s in m.supp))```
	 ```m.Cost = Objective(rule=Min_Cost_Rule, sense=minimize)```

```
Solver Status:

- Status: ok
  Termination condition: optimal
  Statistics:
    Branch and bound:
      Number of bounded subproblems: 0
      Number of created subproblems: 0
  Error rc: 0
  Time: 0.05143117904663086

Optimum Objective Function Value:
1430.03248190070006
```

Figure 4.4: Python Output

Table 4.23: Optimal Results Data Snapshot

Food	Supplier	Amt
Corn Meal	1	50
Corn Meal	2	33
Flour	1	30

4.4   Practice Problems

1. A no-kill animal shelter believes that it will need the following number of volunteers during each one of the next three years: 60 in year 1; 70 in year 2; 50 in year 3. At the beginning of each year, they must decide how many new volunteers to bring on-board and how many to release. It costs \$400 to bring aboard a new volunteer. The shelter expects to pay \$1000 per hired volunteer per year for transportation reimbursement. At the beginning of year 1, the company has 50 volunteers. Determine how to minimize the shelter's cost over the next three years. How is your solution different if the cost to bring aboard a new volunteer increases to \$1200?

2. For the Food Basket Optimization use case, disallow Oatmeal and investigate the resulting optimal solution. You can do this by removing a row from the food input table, removing 'Oatmeal' from the food index set, changing the upper bound on *FoodAmt['Oatmeal']* to 0, or fixing *FoodAmt['Oatmeal']* to 0.

3. For the Food Basket and Delivery Optimization use case, omit the explicit constraint (4.3) and instead impose an upper bound on the $FoodAmt_{f,s}$ variable. In SAS, you can do this in the VAR statement or by modifying the .ub variable suffix. In Python, you can also add an upper bound when defining the variable. Compare the presolved problem statistics from the log before and after this change.

Chapter 5

Mixed Integer Linear Programming

Mixed Integer Linear Programming (MILP) is one of the most widely applied operations research techniques in industry. Most real-world optimization projects require both continuous and discrete decisions. This chapter first reviews MILP concepts and then presents two use cases based on real applications, followed by several practice problems related to these use cases.

5.1   Concepts Review

In Linear Programming (LP) problems, discussed in Chapter 4, the objective function and constraints are required to be linear, and the variables are required to be continuous. If the decision variables instead represent discrete quantities, such as the number of airplanes to produce, the optimization model requires *integer variables*, which must take integer values. An important special case is when a decision variable represents a yes-no decision with possible values 1 and 0, such as whether to build a facility at a candidate location. In this case, the integer variable is called a *binary variable*. An optimization problem that has a linear objective function, all constraints linear, and all variables integer is called an *Integer Linear Programming (ILP) problem*. If the problem instead has both continuous and integer variables, it is called a *Mixed Integer Linear Programming (MILP) problem*. In practice, both ILP and MILP are often referred to collectively as MILP, whether or not any of the variables are continuous.

To solve a MILP problem, the most common algorithm is *branch-and-bound*, introduced by Land and Doig [LD60]. This algorithm implements a dynamic tree search, where the root node of the tree corresponds to the *linear programming relaxation* obtained by temporarily treating all variables as continuous. An LP solver first solves the root node LP. If all integer variables take integer values, we are done, and the algorithm terminates with an optimal solution. Otherwise, a *fractional variable* (integer variable that takes a fractional value in the LP solution) is chosen, and two child nodes are created according to the fractional value. For example, suppose integer variable x_3 takes value 4.2 in the LP solution and is selected as the fractional variable. Then the two child nodes correspond to $x_3 \leq \lfloor 4.2 \rfloor = 4$ and $x_3 \geq \lceil 4.2 \rceil = 5$. This process, called *branching* on x_3, partitions the feasible region into two non-overlapping regions that together contain all integer feasible solutions. Each child node is solved with the additional bound on the branching variable, and the process repeats recursively. For a problem with n variables, all of which are binary, this divide-and-conquer approach could create a tree with $2^{n+1} - 1$ nodes. In practice, a much smaller tree is needed to find and prove an optimal solution, because a node can be *pruned* in three possible ways:

- If there are no fractional variables in the LP solution at the current node, no branching occurs, and the node is *pruned by integrality*.
- If the LP is infeasible at the current node, no branching occurs, and the node is *pruned by infeasibility*.
- If the optimal objective value of the LP at the current node is no better than the *incumbent solution* (best integer feasible solution found so far), no branching occurs, and the node is *pruned by bound*.

The algorithm just described is a simple approach that is sometimes called *vanilla branch-and-bound*. Commercial solvers implement several techniques to improve the overall solve time:

- A *presolver*, invoked before solving the root LP, attempts to reduce the problem size by removing variables and constraints that can be determined to be unnecessary.
- *Cutting planes* (or *cuts*) are constraints that are valid in the sense that every integer feasible solution satisfies them. A *cut generator* attempts to find cuts that are violated by the current fractional solution. Adding these cuts to the problem, especially at the root node, can reduce the amount of

branching needed. The branch-and-bound algorithm with cutting planes is often called *branch-and-cut*.

- *Primal heuristics* attempt to construct good integer feasible solutions, sometimes from scratch and sometimes by modifying existing solutions. Finding solutions early in the search increases the opportunities for pruning by bound.
- *Symmetry detection* avoids performing redundant work when two nodes correspond to essentially the same problem.

For more information about the branch-and-cut algorithm implemented in SAS, see the mixed integer linear programming solver chapter in [SAS23].

An alternative algorithm called *Dantzig-Wolfe decomposition* can sometimes exploit additional problem structures to dramatically improve solve times, and SAS has an automated implementation of this powerful algorithm. For more details, see the decomposition algorithm chapter in [SAS23].

Similar to linear programming problems, in Python, GLPK can also solve mixed integer linear problems [dt12].

For in-depth information about mixed integer linear models and solution algorithms, please refer to [BW05] or [Wol20].

5.2 Use Case: Optimizing K-5 Student Schedules During COVID-19

During the COVID-19 pandemic that began in Spring 2020, public and private schools struggled to design how to best bring students back for face-to-face instruction (if bringing them back at all). Health risks to students and teachers, working parents struggling (i.e., losing their cool) with child-care options, school capacities, and budget limitations, among many others, made this problem a logistical nightmare. Even without the emotional and political implications, timetabling (this type of scheduling problem) is a concept that would instill fear in the bravest operations research practitioner. Given this complexity, most schools began classes virtually. However, for many students, particularly the youngest ones, being in a face-to-face environment and having direct teacher-led instruction best fit their learning style and academic needs. The goal of this formulation was to recommend a schedule that maximized the amount of face-to-face instruction while respecting state and federal guidelines, school capacities, and logistical constraints.

The following problem definition is a simplified version of the original problem that the SAS Analytics Center of Excellence (Subramanian Pazhani, Matt Fletcher, Lee Ellen Harmer, and Natalia Summerville) developed in partnership with Durham Public Schools (Matthew Palmer) in 2020. More details can be found in [Sum20] and [Paz20].

5.2.1   Problem Definition

We must decide how many students to allocate to each classroom (decision variables) such that the total amount of face-to-face instruction time is maximized (objective function). Maximum classroom capacity as recommended by CDC cannot be exceeded (constraint), students across grades must have the same number of instructional hours (constraint), and students across grades cannot be mixed in the same classroom at the same time (constraint).

5.2.2   Data and Settings Inputs

The required data include student population per grade (data input) and physical capacity of each room (data input). The user also needs to specify parameters such as time block granularity or number of hours per time block (settings input), daily start and end times (settings input), and allowed percent capacity (settings input). This use case uses data for Lakewood Elementary School.

The data dictionary in Table 5.1 contains more detailed information about the tables and the variables.

Table 5.1: Data Dictionary			
Data Table	Variable Name	Variable Type	Variable Description
INPUT_GRADES	Grade_ID	Char	Unique ID for school grade
INPUT_GRADES	Population	Num	Total grade population (number of students)
INPUT_ROOMS	Room_ID	Char	Unique ID for classroom
INPUT_ROOMS	Capacity	Num	Total classroom capacity (number of students)
INPUT_SETTINGS	Setting_Name	Char	Name of the configuration setting (e.g., MAX_ROOM_CAPACITY, START_TIME)
INPUT_SETTINGS	Setting_Value	Num	Value of the configuration setting (e.g., 50%, 8am)
INPUT_SETTINGS	Setting_Desc	Char	Description of the configuration setting

Tables 5.2 and 5.3 show snapshots of the input data.

Table 5.2: INPUT_GRADES Data Snapshot

Grade_ID	Population
PreK	36
Kindergarden	60
First	59

Table 5.3: INPUT_ROOMS Data Snapshot

Room_ID	Capacity
A121	30
A120	26
A123	30

5.2.3   Mathematical Formulation

User-defined Settings

Table 5.4 shows the user-defined settings that come from the INPUT_SETTINGS tables and are considered constants in the mathematical model.

Table 5.4: User-defined Settings	
Setting Name	Setting Description
maxPctCapacity	Maximum percentage of capacity allowed
hrsBlock	Number of hours in each time block
startTime	Daily start time
endTime	Daily end time

Calculated Setting

Table 5.5 shows the setting that is calculated from other input settings and is considered constant in the mathematical model.

Table 5.5: Calculated Setting	
Setting Name and Formula	Setting Description
$numBlocks = \dfrac{endTime - startTime}{hrsBlock}$	Number of time blocks per day

Dimensions

The dimensions relevant in this use case are the grades, rooms, and time blocks, as shown in Table 5.6.

Table 5.6: Dimensions	
Dimension Name	Dimension Description
$g \in$ GRADES	Set of grades
$r \in$ ROOMS	Set of rooms
$b \in$ BLOCKS	Set of time blocks

Data Parameters

The capacity per room and population per grade are the main data inputs from the INPUT_GRADES and INPUT_ROOMS tables, as shown in Table 5.7.

Table 5.7: Data Parameters	
Parameter Name	Parameter Description
$capacity_r$	Physical capacity of each room r
$population_g$	Number of students in grade g

Decision Variables

The key decision variables are the number of students to allocate to each grade, room, and time block, and a binary variable to indicate whether that allocation is positive, as shown in Table 5.8.

Table 5.8: Decision Variables	
Variable Name	Variable Description
$NumStudents_{g,r,b}$	Number of students from grade g in room r in block b
$Assign_{g,r,b}$	Binary variable to indicate assignment of grade g to room r in block b

Constraints

This use case imposes the following constraints:

$$NumStudents_{g,r,b} \leq maxPctCapacity \times capacity_r \quad \text{for all } g, r, b \quad (5.1)$$

$$Assign_{g,r,b} \leq NumStudents_{g,r,b} \quad \text{for all } g, r, b \quad (5.2)$$

$$population_g \times Assign_{g,r,b} \geq NumStudents_{g,r,b} \quad \text{for all } g, r, b \quad (5.3)$$

$$\sum_g Assign_{g,r,b} \leq 1 \quad \text{for all } r, b \quad (5.4)$$

$$\sum_{r,b} Assign_{g,r,b} \leq \frac{\sum_{g_1,r,b} Assign_{g_1,r,b}}{|\text{GRADES}|} + 1 \quad \text{for all } g \quad (5.5)$$

Constraint (5.1) is to not exceed the reduced room capacity in terms of number of students.

To guarantee that students from different grades are not mixed in one classroom at the same time, we introduced an auxiliary binary variable to indicate whether a grade is assigned to a room in a time block. To make sure that this auxiliary variable takes the value of 0 if no students from that grade are assigned, and the value of 1 if any students from that grade are assigned, we use a big-M value (the population for grade g) and impose constraints (5.2) and (5.3). More recommendations on the big-M formulation are detailed in the Tips and Tricks section later in this chapter.

Constraint (5.4) makes sure that only one grade is assigned per room per time block.

In this use case, we also want to balance the student assignments to blocks and rooms (as a proxy for total face-to-face time) across grades, making sure the face-to-face time is not disproportional for one grade versus another. Constraint (5.5) enforces this balance across grades, allowing for at most one time block difference between grades.

Objective Function

The objective in this use case is to maximize student face-to-face instruction time:

$$\max\; TotalStudentHours = hrsBlock \times \sum_{g,r,b} NumStudents_{g,r,b}$$

5.2.4   Mathematical Formulation and SAS Model

Tables 5.9 and 5.10 show the mathematical formulation and the corresponding SAS code. The full code can be found in the supporting materials.

Table 5.9: SAS Code for Sets, Parameters, and Variables	
MATHEMATICS	SAS CODE
$maxPctCapacity$	`num maxPctCapacity;`
$hrsBlock$	`num hrsBlock;`
$startTime$	`num startTime;`
$endTime$	`num endTime;`
$numBlocks = \dfrac{endTime - startTime}{hrsBlock}$	`num numBlocks = (endTime - startTime) / hrsBlock;`
$g \in \text{GRADES}$	`set <str> GRADES;`
$r \in \text{ROOMS}$	`set <str> ROOMS;`
$b \in \text{BLOCKS}$	`set BLOCKS = 1..numBlocks;`
$capacity_r$	`num capacity {ROOMS};`
$population_g$	`num population {GRADES};`
$NumStudents_{g,r,b}$	`var NumStudents {GRADES, ROOMS, BLOCKS} >= 0 integer;`
$Assign_{g,r,b}$	`var Assign {GRADES, ROOMS, BLOCKS} binary;`

Table 5.10: SAS Code for Constraints and Objective Function

MATHEMATICS	SAS CODE
$NumStudents_{g,r,b} \leq maxPctCapacity \times capacity_r$ for all g,r,b	```con LimitedRoomCapacity {g in GRADES, r in ROOMS, b in BLOCKS}:``` ``` NumStudents[g,r,b] <= maxPctCapacity * capacity[r];```
$Assign_{g,r,b} \leq NumStudents_{g,r,b}$ for all g,r,b	```con DefineAssign1 {g in GRADES, r in ROOMS, b in BLOCKS}:``` ``` Assign[g,r,b] <= NumStudents[g,r,b];```
$population_g \times Assign_{g,r,b} \geq NumStudents_{g,r,b}$ for all g,r,b	```con DefineAssign2 {g in GRADES, r in ROOMS, b in BLOCKS}:``` ``` population[g] * Assign[g,r,b] >= NumStudents[g,r,b];```
$\sum_g Assign_{g,r,b} \leq 1$ for all r,b	```con OneGradePerRoomBlock {r in ROOMS, b in BLOCKS}:``` ``` sum {g in GRADES} Assign[g,r,b] <= 1;```

$\sum_{r,b} Assign_{g,r,b} \leq \dfrac{\sum_{g_1,r,b} Assign_{g_1,r,b}}{\|GRADES\|} + 1$ for all g	```con BalanceHoursGrades {g in GRADES}:```
	``` sum {r in ROOMS, b in BLOCKS} Assign[g,r,b]```
	``` <= (sum {g1 in GRADES, r in ROOMS, b in BLOCKS}```
	``` Assign[g1,r,b]) / card(GRADES) + 1;```

$\max TotalStudentHours = hrsBlock \times \sum_{g,r,b} NumStudents_{g,r,b}$	```max TotalStudentHours = hrsBlock *``` ``` sum {g in GRADES, r in ROOMS, b in BLOCKS} NumStudents[g,r,b];```

5.2.5   SAS Output

Figure 5.1 shows the Solution Summary produced by the SAS code, including the optimum value for the objective function.

The SAS System

The OPTMODEL Procedure

Solution Summary	
Solver	MILP
Algorithm	Branch and Cut
Objective Function	TotalStudentHours
Solution Status	Optimal
Objective Value	1328
Relative Gap	0
Absolute Gap	0
Primal Infeasibility	0
Bound Infeasibility	0
Integer Infeasibility	0
Best Bound	1328
Nodes	1
Solutions Found	8
Iterations	951
Presolve Time	0.04
Solution Time	0.14

Figure 5.1: SAS Output

5.2.6   Mathematical Formulation and Python Model

Tables 5.11 and 5.12 show the mathematical formulation and the corresponding Python code. The full code can be found in the supporting materials.

Table 5.11: Python Code for Sets, Parameters, and Variables

MATHEMATICS	PYTHON CODE
maxPctCapacity	`m.maxPctCapacity=Param()`
hrsBlock	`m.hrsBlock=Param()`
startTime	`m.startTime=Param()`
endTime	`m.endTime=Param()`
$numBlocks = \dfrac{endTime - startTime}{hrsBlock}$	`m.numBlocks=` `  Param(initialize=(m.endTime-m.startTime)/(m.hrsBlock))`
$g \in$ GRADES	`m.grades = Set()`
$r \in$ ROOMS	`m.rooms = Set()`
$b \in$ BLOCKS	`m.blocks = RangeSet(1,m.numBlocks)`
$capacity_r$	`m.capacity=Param(m.rooms)`
$population_g$	`m.population=Param(m.grades)`
$NumStudents_{g,r,b}$	`m.NumStudents=` `  Var(m.grades,m.rooms,m.blocks,domain=NonNegativeIntegers)`
$Assign_{g,r,b}$	`m.Assign=Var(m.grades,m.rooms,m.blocks,domain=Binary)`

Table 5.12: Python Code for Constraints and Objective Function

$NumStudents_{g,r,b} \leq maxPctCapacity \times capacity_r$ for all g, r, b

```python
def LimitedRoomCapacity(m,g,r,b):
    return m.NumStudents[g,r,b] <= m.maxPctCapacity*m.capacity[r]
m.LimitedRoomCapacity =
    Constraint(m.grades, m.rooms, m.blocks, rule=LimitedRoomCapacity)
```

$Assign_{g,r,b} \leq NumStudents_{g,r,b}$ for all g, r, b

```python
def DefineAssign1(m,g,r,b):
    return m.Assign[g,r,b] <= m.NumStudents[g,r,b]
m.DefineAssign1 =
    Constraint(m.grades, m.rooms, m.blocks, rule=DefineAssign1)
```

$population_g \times Assign_{g,r,b} \geq NumStudents_{g,r,b}$ for all g, r, b

```python
def DefineAssign2(m,g,r,b):
    return m.population[g]*m.Assign[g,r,b] >= m.NumStudents[g,r,b]
m.DefineAssign2 =
    Constraint(m.grades, m.rooms, m.blocks, rule=DefineAssign2)
```

$\sum_g Assign_{g,r,b} \leq 1$ for all r, b

```python
def OneGradePerRoomBlock(m,r,b):
    return sum(m.Assign[g,r,b] for g in m.grades) <= 1
m.OneGradePerRoomBlock =
    Constraint(m.rooms, m.blocks, rule=OneGradePerRoomBlock)
```

$$\sum_{g_1,r,b} Assign_{g_1,r,b} \leq \frac{\sum_{r,b} Assign_{g,r,b}}{|GRADES|} + 1 \text{ for all } g$$

```python
def BalanceHoursGrades(m,g):
    return (sum(m.Assign[g,r,b] for r in m.rooms for b in m.blocks) -
    (sum(m.Assign[g1,r,b] for g1 in m.grades for r in m.rooms
    for b in m.blocks))/len(m.grades)) <= 1
m.BalanceHoursGrades = Constraint(m.grades, rule=BalanceHoursGrades)
```

max $TotalStudentHours = hrsBlock \times \sum_{g,r,b} NumStudents_{g,r,b}$

```python
def TotalStudentHours(m):
    return sum(m.hrsBlock*m.NumStudents[g,r,b]
    for g in m.grades for r in m.rooms for b in m.blocks)
m.TotalStudentHours = Objective(rule=TotalStudentHours, sense=maximize)
```

5.2.7   Python Output

Figure 5.2 shows the output produced by the Python code, including the optimum value for the objective function.

```
Solver Status:

- Status: ok
  Termination condition: optimal
  Statistics:
    Branch and bound:
      Number of bounded subproblems: 281
      Number of created subproblems: 281
  Error rc: 0
  Time: 0.33526611328125

Optimum Objective Function Value:
1328.0
```

Figure 5.2: Python Output

5.2.8   Output Results

Table 5.13 shows a snapshot of the optimal results. This is the number of students in each cohort that is defined by grade, room, and time block.

Table 5.13: Optimal Results Data Snapshot

Grade	Room	Time Block	NumStudents
PreK	A120	4	13
PreK	A137	1	12
PreK	A137	4	12

5.3   Use Case: Optimizing Breast Milk Donation Collection Sites

Mothers' Milk Bank, a milk bank partnered with WakeMed, is part of the Human Milk Banking Association of North America (HMBANA). Mothers' Milk Bank screens donors before accepting milk donations. When donations are received, further processing is completed through milk pooling, pasteurizing, and bacterial testing before dispensing the milk to clients. They serve Newborn Intensive Care Units (NICUs) and birthing centers in 44 hospitals throughout 8 states. Mothers' Milk Bank sources milk donations from various states in the country with a higher concentration of donations originating in North Carolina.

The following problem definition is a simplified version of the original problem that NCSU Industrial Engineering students (Jenny Breese, Diego Hernandez, Sean Murray, John Schell, and Conner Walker), under the advising of NCSU Lecturer Natalia Summerville, developed in partnership with Mothers' Milk Bank (Montana Wagner-Gillespie) in 2018. More information can be found in [Alb20] and [Las19].

5.3.1   Problem Definition

The Milk Bank in Cary, NC, has one depot site where donors can drop off their milk. If donors do not have a drop-off location nearby, Mothers' Milk Bank will pay for overnight breast milk shipping for the donor, therefore incurring high shipping costs. Mothers' Milk Bank believed introducing additional collection sites would increase its reach and potentially reduce cost. These added depot sites might be open year-round or seasonally.

To support Mothers' Milk Bank, an optimization model was built to decide where and how many collection sites to place (decision variables), minimizing the overall shipping distance multiplied by the total shipped weight as a proxy for shipping cost (objective function) for donors who do not have a location close by. We assume that donors will decide to ship instead of driving to the collection site if the driving distance is more than a predefined number of miles (constraint), and no more than a certain number of sites can be opened (constraint). Because the bank will accept and accommodate all breast milk donations as long as the donor is screened and approved, we do not consider capacity constraints. We also do not consider collection sites building costs since it typically only requires a freezer and is operated by volunteers.

5.3.2 Data and Settings Inputs

The required data include the donor locations as a ZIP code (data input), their typical (historical) number of shipments (data input), and typical shipment weight (data input). We also need to obtain the locations of the potential drop-off collection sites (data input), which are mostly clinics and hospitals that are willing to put a collection site in their locations. The distance between each donor and each potential collection site (data input) is also provided. Finally, the user also needs to provide the maximum number of sites that can be placed (settings input) as well as the maximum distance a donor is willing to travel for the drop-off (settings input). A detailed data dictionary is shown in Table 5.14.

Table 5.14: Data Dictionary			
Data Table	Variable Name	Variable Type	Variable Description
INPUT_DONORZIP	DonorZip	Num	Donor ZIP code
INPUT_DONORZIP	donorShip	Num	Typical number of shipments in a time period
INPUT_DONORZIP	weight	Num	Typical weight for a shipment in a time period
INPUT_DROPOFFZIP	dropoff	Num	ZIP code for a possible collection site
INPUT_DISTANCES	donor	Num	Donor ZIP code
INPUT_DISTANCES	dropoff	Num	ZIP code for a possible collection site
INPUT_DISTANCES	distance	Num	Distance between the donor and the possible collection site
INPUT_SETTINGS	Setting_Name	Char	Name of the configuration setting (i.e., MAX_DISTANCE)
INPUT_SETTINGS	Setting_Value	Num	Value of the configuration setting (e.g., 20)
INPUT_SETTINGS	Setting_Desc	Char	Description of the configuration setting

Tables 5.15, 5.16, and 5.17 show snapshots of the input data.

Table 5.15: INPUT_DONORZIP Data Snapshot

DonorZip	Weight	DonorShip
27007	35.125	6
27054	25.125	2
27103	68.0625	10

Table 5.16: INPUT_DROPOFFZIP Data Snapshot

DropOff
27103
27312
27405

Table 5.17: INPUT_DISTANCES Data Snapshot

Donor	DropOff	Distance
27007	27103	43.6009
27007	27312	106.3164
27007	27405	67.594

5.3.3   Mathematical Formulation

User-defined Settings

Table 5.18 shows the user-defined settings that come from the INPUT_SETTINGS table and are considered constants in the mathematical model.

Table 5.18: User-defined Settings	
Setting Name	Setting Description
maxDistance	Maximum distance a donor is willing to travel for a drop-off location
maxNumSites	Maximum number of drop-off sites the Milk Bank can add

Dimensions

The dimensions relevant in this use case are the donor locations and drop-off sites, as shown in Table 5.19.

Table 5.19: Dimensions	
Dimension Name	Dimension Description
$d \in$ DONORS	Set of donor locations
$s \in$ SITES	Set of drop-off sites

Data Parameters

The capacity per room and population per grade are the main data inputs from the INPUT_GRADES and INPUT_ROOMS tables, as shown in Table 5.20.

Table 5.20: Data Parameters	
Parameter Name	Parameter Description
$distance_{d,s}$	Distance from donor d to site s
$weight_d$	Average monthly weight typically shipped from donor location d
$amount_d$	Average amount typically shipped from donor location d

Decision Variables

The key decision variables are a binary variable indicating whether a particular drop-off location is to be open and an auxiliary binary variable to keep track of which donor locations are assigned to the drop-off locations to be open, as shown in Table 5.21.

Table 5.21: Decision Variables	
Variable Name	Variable Description
$Open_s$	Binary variable to indicate whether site s is open
$Assign_{d,s}$	Binary variable to indicate whether donor location d is assigned to site location s

Constraints

This use case imposes the following constraints:

$$\sum_{s} Assign_{d,s} \leq 1 \qquad\qquad \text{for all } d \qquad (5.6)$$

$$\sum_{d} Assign_{d,s} \geq Open_{s} \qquad\qquad \text{for all } s \qquad (5.7)$$

$$\sum_{d} Assign_{d,s} \leq |\text{DONORS}| \times Open_{s} \qquad \text{for all } s \qquad (5.8)$$

$$\sum_{s} distance_{d,s} \times Assign_{d,s} \leq maxDistance \qquad \text{for all } d \qquad (5.9)$$

$$\sum_{s} Open_{s} \leq maxNumSites \qquad\qquad \text{for all } d \qquad (5.10)$$

Constraint (5.6) is to assign at most one drop-off site to each donor.

To guarantee that we open only sites that have donors assigned to them, we introduced an auxiliary binary variable to indicate whether a donor is assigned to a site. To make sure that this auxiliary variable takes the value of 0 if no donors are assigned, and the value of 1 if any donors are assigned, we use a big-M value (the total number of donors) and impose constraints (5.7) and (5.8). More recommendations on the big-M formulation are detailed in the Tips and Tricks section.

Constraint (5.9) assigns donors only to sites that are within the maximum travel distance.

Constraint (5.10) makes sure that no more than the maximum allowed number of sites are open.

Objective Function

The objective in this use case is to minimize the total shipments-distance (weight times amount times distance) for donors not assigned to a new drop-off location:

$$\min\ TotalWeightedDistance$$

$$= \sum_d distance_{d,27609} \times weight_d \times amount_d \times \left(1 - \sum_s Assign_{d,s}\right)$$

5.3.4 Mathematical Formulation and SAS Model

Tables 5.22 and 5.23 show the mathematical formulation and the corresponding SAS code. The full code can be found in the supporting materials.

Table 5.22: SAS Code for Sets, Parameters, and Variables	
MATHEMATICS	SAS CODE
$maxDistance$	`num maxDistance;`
$maxNumSites$	`num maxNumSites;`
$d \in$ DONORS	`set DONORS;`
$s \in$ SITES	`set SITES;`
$distance_{d,s}$	`num distance {DONORS, SITES};`
$weight_d$	`num weight {DONORS};`
$amount_d$	`num amount {DONORS};`
$Open_s$	`var Open {SITES} binary;`
$Assign_{d,s}$	`var Assign {DONORS, SITES} binary;`

Table 5.23: SAS Code for Constraints and Objective Function

MATHEMATICS	SAS CODE
$\sum_s Assign_{d,s} \leq 1$ for all d	```con Assign_Once {d in DONORS}:``` ```sum {s in SITES} Assign[d,s] <= 1;```
$\sum_d Assign_{d,s} \geq Open_s$ for all s	```con If_NotAssigned_Then_Closed {s in SITES}:``` ```sum {d in DONORS} Assign[d,s] >= Open[s];```
$\sum_d Assign_{d,s} \leq \lvert DONORS \rvert \times Open_s$ for all s	```con If_Assigned_Then_Open {s in SITES}:``` ```sum {d in DONORS} Assign[d,s] <= card(DONORS) * Open[s];```
$\sum_s distance_{d,s} \times Assign_{d,s} \leq$ $maxDistance$ for all d	```con Distance_Traveled {d in DONORS}:``` ```sum {s in SITES} distance[d,s] * Assign[d,s] <= maxDistance;```
$\sum_s Open_s \leq maxNumSites$	```con Only_Open_N_Sites:``` ```sum {s in SITES} Open[s] <= maxNumSites;```

min $TotalWeightedDistance =$ $\sum_d distance_{d,27609} \times weight_d \times amount_d \times$ $(1 - \sum_s Assign_{d,s})$	```min TotalWeightedDistance =```
	 ```sum {d in DONORS} distance[d,27609] * weight[d] * amount[d] *```
	 ```(1 - sum {s in SITES} Assign[d,s]);```

5.3.5 SAS Output

Figure 5.3 shows the Solution Summary produced by the SAS code, including the optimum value for the objective function.

The SAS System

The OPTMODEL Procedure

Solution Summary	
Solver	MILP
Algorithm	Branch and Cut
Objective Function	TotalWeightedDistance
Solution Status	Optimal
Objective Value	8513904.3346
Relative Gap	0
Absolute Gap	0
Primal Infeasibility	2.220446E-16
Bound Infeasibility	2.220446E-16
Integer Infeasibility	1.199041E-14
Best Bound	8513904.3346
Nodes	1
Solutions Found	7
Iterations	2018
Presolve Time	0.02
Solution Time	0.22

Figure 5.3: SAS Output

5.3.6   Mathematical Formulation and Python Model

Tables 5.24 and 5.25 show the mathematical formulation and the corresponding Python code. The full code can be found in the supporting materials.

Table 5.24: Python Code for Sets, Parameters, and Variables

MATHEMATICS	PYTHON CODE
$maxDistance$	`m.maxDistance = Param()`
$maxNumSites$	`m.maxNumSites = Param()`
$d \in \text{DONORS}$	`m.donors = Set()`
$s \in \text{SITES}$	`m.sites = Set()`
$distance_{d,s}$	`m.distance = Param(m.donors,m.sites)`
$weight_d$	`m.weight = Param(m.donors)`
$amount_d$	`m.amount = Param(m.donors)`
$Open_s$	`m.Open = Var(m.sites, domain = Binary)`
$Assign_{d,s}$	`m.Assign = Var(m.donors, m.sites, domain = Binary)`

Table 5.25: Python Code for Constraints and Objective Function

Math	Python Code
$\sum_s Assign_{d,s} \leq 1$ for all d	```def Assign_Once(m,d):\n return sum(m.Assign[d,s] for s in m.sites)<=1\nm.Assign_Once = Constraint(m.donors, rule=Assign_Once)```
$\sum_d Assign_{d,s} \geq Open_s$ for all s	```def If_NotAssigned_Then_Closed(m,s):\n return sum(m.Assign[d,s] for d in m.donors) >= m.Open[s]\nm.If_NotAssigned_Then_Closed =\nConstraint(m.sites, rule=If_NotAssigned_Then_Closed)```
$\sum_d Assign_{d,s} \leq$ $|DONORS| \times Open_s$ for all s	```def If_Assigned_Then_Open(m,s):\n return sum(m.Assign[d,s] for d in m.donors) <= len(m.donors)*m.Open[s]\nm.If_Assigned_Then_Open =\nConstraint(m.sites, rule=If_Assigned_Then_Open)```
$\sum_s distance_{d,s} \times Assign_{d,s} \leq$ $maxDistance$ for all d	```def Distance_Traveled(m,d):\n return sum(m.distance[d,s]*m.Assign[d,s] for s in m.sites) <=\nm.maxDistance\nm.Distance_Traveled = Constraint(m.donors, rule=Distance_Traveled)```
$\sum_s Open_s \leq maxNumSites$	```def Only_Open_N_Sites(m):\n return sum(m.Open[s] for s in m.sites) <= m.maxNumSites\nm.Only_Open_N_Sites = Constraint(rule=Only_Open_N_Sites)```
min $TotalWeightedDistance =$ $\sum_d distance_{d,27609} \times weight_d \times$ $amount_d \times (1 - \sum_s Assign_{d,s})$	```def Total_Weighted_Distance(m):\n return sum(m.distance[d,27609]*m.weight[d]*m.amount[d]*\n(1-sum(m.Assign[d,s] for s in m.sites)) for d in m.donors)\nm.Total_Weighted_Distance =\nObjective(rule=Total_Weighted_Distance, sense=minimize)```

5.3.7 Python Output

Figure 5.4 shows the output produced by the Python code, including the optimum value for the objective function.

```
Solver Status:

- Status: ok
  Termination condition: optimal
  Statistics:
    Branch and bound:
      Number of bounded subproblems: 3921
      Number of created subproblems: 3921
  Error rc: 0
  Time: 0.8281762599945068

Optimum Objective Function Value:
8513904.334555969
```

Figure 5.4: Python Output

5.3.8 Output Results

Table 5.26 shows a snapshot of the optimal results., which is the assignment of donor ZIP codes to donation sites that are suggested to be built.

Table 5.26: Optimal Results Data Snapshot

Donor Zipcode	DropOff Zipcode
27502	27518
27510	27707
27511	27518

5.4 Tips and Tricks

5.4.1 *Big-M* Formulation and Auxiliary Binary Variables

Often in MILP applications we need to add auxiliary binary decision variables to represent the business problem accurately, and those auxiliary variables sometimes require a *big-M* formulation. Suppose you have a binary variable y and want to enforce a logical implication

$$f(x) > b \implies y = 1,$$

equivalently, its contrapositive,

$$y = 0 \implies f(x) \le b.$$

Some optimization modeling languages, including OPTMODEL in SAS, support the use of indicator constraints to express the logical implication directly. Otherwise, you can introduce a constant big-M value M and impose a linear constraint

$$f(x) - b \le My.$$

Then $y = 0$ would imply that $f(x) - b \le 0$, as desired, and $y = 1$ would imply $f(x) - b \le M$, where you choose M so that this latter constraint is redundant. Occasionally, optimization practitioners use an arbitrarily large value like $M = 99999$, but a best practice is to use a data-dependent value instead. A value that is too large will introduce numerical difficulties, and a value that is too small will cut off feasible solutions. An ideal choice for M is a tight upper bound on the left-hand side $f(x) - b$ when $y = 1$.

In our School Optimization use case, we generated a binary variable called $Assign_{g,r,b}$ that was required to guarantee that students from different classrooms were not assigned to the same room and time block. To have this variable take the value of 1 when any students from grade g were assigned to the corresponding room r and block b, we introduced a *big-M* type of formulation, setting the *big-M* value to $population_g$. An alternative value of *big-M* could be $\sum_g population_g$, but this value would not be as tight as the original definition, which will potentially translate into longer run-times (and we, OR practitioners, don't like long run-times!).

5.4.2 Logical Implication Between Two Binary Variables

An implication that often arises when binary variables represent yes-no decisions is

$$x = 1 \implies y = 1.$$

That is, if the decision represented by x is yes, then the decision represented by y is also yes. For example, if you assign a customer to a facility, you must open the facility. You can enforce this relation via an indicator constraint or by explicitly imposing a linear constraint

$$x \leq y.$$

If $x = 1$, this constraint forces $1 \leq y$, equivalently, $y = 1$. If $x = 0$, then y can take either value (0 or 1), as desired. Note that this formulation is a special case of the previous section that arises by taking $f(x) = x$, $b = 0$, and $M = 1$.

5.5   Practice Problems

1. In treating a brain tumor with radiation, physicians want the maximum amount of radiation possible to bombard the tissue containing the tumors. The constraint is, however, that there is a maximum amount of radiation that normal tissue can handle without suffering tissue damage. Physicians must therefore decide how to aim the radiation to maximize the radiation that hits the tumor tissue while not damaging the normal tissue. As a simple example of this situation, suppose there are three types of radiation beams (beams differ in where they are aimed and their intensity) that can be aimed at a tumor. The region containing the tumor has been divided into four regions: two regions contain normal tissue (regions 1 and 2), and two contain tumors (regions 3 and 4). The amount of radiation delivered to each region by each type of beam is shown in Table 5.27. If each region of normal tissue can handle at most 40 units of radiation, which beams should be used to maximize the total amount of radiation received by the tumors? (Adapted from *Business Analytics: Data Analysis & Decision Making, Sixth Edition*, by S. Christian Albright and Wayne L. Winston.)

Table 5.27: Data for problem 1

Beam	Region 1	Region 2	Region 3	Region 4
1	24	18	12	30
2	18	15	9	27
3	14	12	20	20

2. USP Media needs to decide how many spots (30-second commercials) to schedule in each one of the four available TV shows during a two-day planning period for its main customer, Tesma. USP does not allow

more than three spots in the same TV show/same day for a given customer. Tesma has requested to reach at least 50 million male users 30–50 years old with the overall advertisement plan. Tesma's budget is $1,000,000. The available TV shows, their cost (thousands of dollars per one spot), and expected audience (millions per one spot) are provided in MILP_P2_media_cost_audience.csv data.

(a) Build an advertisement plan that minimizes the deviation from the available budget.
(b) What is the expected audience reach with this plan?
(c) What is the deviation from budget with this plan?

3. For the K-5 Student Schedule use case, how much would the total face-to-face instruction time increase if we allowed up to one hour of difference in the face-to-face time each grade has? That is, if Grade 1 has two face-to-face hours then Grade 2 could have between one and three hours.

4. For the Mothers' Milk use case, update the objective function to minimize the number of new sites (instead of minimizing distance × weight × amount), but do not allow the total distance × weight × amount to exceed 8 million.

5. For the Mothers' Milk use case, evaluate the improvement in run time by reducing the number of variables, removing the combinations of donor/drop-off that exceed the allowed distance.

6. For the Mothers' Milk use case, evaluate the difference in run time by disaggregating the big-M constraint (5.8) as $Assign_{d,s} \leq Open_s$ for all d and s.

Chapter 6

Nonlinear Programming

Some real-world optimization problems naturally involve nonlinear relationships among decision variables. For example, revenue maximization can involve the product of two decision variables, one representing price and one representing the expected sales as a decreasing function of price. This chapter first reviews nonlinear programming (NLP) concepts and then presents two use cases based on real applications, followed by several practice problems related to these use cases.

6.1 Concepts Review

A *Nonlinear Programming (NLP) problem* is an optimization problem where all the variables are continuous, and where the objective function and/or some constraint(s) are not linear. It should be highlighted that if not all variables are continuous, the problem would be *Mixed Integer Nonlinear Programming (MINLP)* and you are in for a big headache. This chapter discusses NLP only. In mathematical notation, the problem is to maximize or minimize a function $f(x_1, \ldots, x_n)$ subject to constraints $g_i(x_1, \ldots, x_n) = b_i$ for $i \in \{1, \ldots, m\}$ and $\ell_j \leq x_j \leq u_j$ for $j \in \{1, \ldots, n\}$. Here, f is the *objective function*, the g_i functions are *constraint functions*, b_i is the *right-hand side*, and ℓ_j and u_j are *lower and upper bounds*, respectively, for the decision variable x_j. Commonly, the decision variables represent physical quantities for which $\ell_j = 0$ and $u_j = \infty$, but either bound can be finite or infinite. For simplicity, the notation used here expresses each constraint as an equality, but most NLP solvers accept any combination of $=$, $\leq$, and $\geq$ constraints.

To solve an NLP problem, two alternative algorithms are common:

- The *active-set algorithm* considers all equality constraints and a subset of inequality constraints in each iteration. This approach can be helpful since by temporarily ignoring some of the inequality constraints, the overall computational time can be reduced.
- The *interior point algorithm* can be efficient for large-scale NLPs, in part because it can naturally use parallel processing.

SAS provides both of these NLP algorithms, and interior point is the default. A *concurrent* option can run the active-set and interior point algorithms simultaneously on multiple threads, returning an optimal solution whenever the first algorithm finishes. Both algorithms return a *locally optimal* solution that is feasible and has a better objective value than any nearby solution. In contrast, a *globally optimal* solution is feasible and has the best possible objective value among all solutions, nearby or not. A *multistart* option can improve the likelihood of finding a globally optimal solution for problems that have many locally optimal solutions. For more information about the NLP solver in SAS, see the nonlinear programming solver chapter in [SAS23].

In Python, one of the most used nonlinear programming solvers is IPOPT [dt22a].

For in-depth information about nonlinear models and solution algorithms, please refer to [BSS13].

6.2 Use Case: Optimizing Seed Placement in Prostate Brachytherapy

Radiation therapy for prostate cancer can be delivered by brachytherapy (permanent implantation of radioactive seeds or high dose rate treatment). In brachytherapy, radioactive sources (Iodine-125 or Palladium-103) are permanently implanted in the prostate in a pattern designed to maximize the dose to the tumor while avoiding overexposure of the surrounding normal tissues. A major limitation of radioactive-seed implants has been the difficulty of accurately placing 60–150 seeds within the prostate in a specified geometric pattern. If a seed is placed in a specific location, then it contributes a certain amount of radiation dosage to each point in the area to be treated. Lower and upper bounds for dose to all structures are predefined.

The following use case is a simplified application based on the extended research performed for the Memorial Sloan Kettering Cancer Center [LZ08], which won the 2007 Franz Edelman Award for Achievement in Advanced Analytics, Operations Research, and Management Science from INFORMS.

We would also like to mention that Memorial Sloan Kettering Cancer Center researchers were again Franz Edelman Award finalists in 2021 for their work in Medical Physics, this time improving radiotherapy with high-energy photon beams placement optimization [ZHZ+22].

6.2.1   Problem Definition

In optimization terms, we need to decide where to place the seeds, such that the exposure of the healthy tissues is minimized while achieving the target exposure for tumor tissue. We solve this problem by minimizing the maximum exposure across all points subject to a lower bound on exposure for tumorous points. The contribution equation is a nonlinear function of the distance from the seed to the point, effectively making this a nonlinear optimization problem.

The radiation exposure is typically inversely proportional to the square root of the distance [BFG+01]. However, for illustration and simplicity purposes of this example, we define it as inversely proportional to the distance and represent it as follows:

$$Exposure = \frac{1}{Distance}$$

6.2.2   Data and Settings Inputs

The required data include all the predefined points where the exposure is going to be measured, their x and y coordinates, and classification as healthy or tumorous tissue (data input). We also need to specify parameters such as the number of seeds to be placed (user input) and target radiation exposure (user input).

The data dictionary in Table 6.1 contains more detailed information about the tables and the variables.

Table 6.1: Data Dictionary			
Data Table	Variable Name	Variable Type	Variable Description
INPUT_POINTS	Point_ID	Num	Unique ID for each point
INPUT_POINTS	X_Coord	Num	X coordinate
INPUT_POINTS	Y_Coord	Num	Y coordinate
INPUT_POINTS	Tumor_Flg	Num	1 if this point has tumorous tissue, 0 otherwise
INPUT_SETTINGS	Setting_Name	Char	Name of the configuration setting (e.g., Num_Seeds)
INPUT_SETTINGS	Setting_Value	Num	Value of the configuration setting (e.g., 4)

Tables 6.2 and 6.3 show snapshots of the input data. Figure 6.1 shows a heat map of the tumorous tissue, red zones representing tumor tissue and blue zones healthy tissue.

Table 6.2: INPUT_POINTS Data Snapshot

Point_ID	X_Coord	Y_Coord	Tumor_Flg
1	1	1	0
2	1	2	1
3	1	3	0

Table 6.3: INPUT_SETTINGS Data Snapshot

Setting_Name	Setting_Value
NumSeeds	3
TargetTumorExp	3

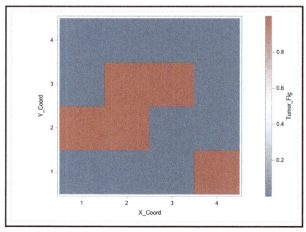

Figure 6.1: Heat Map of Tumorous Tissue

6.2.3   Mathematical Formulation

User-defined Settings

Table 6.4 shows the user-defined settings that come from the INPUT_SETTINGS table and are considered constants in the mathematical model.

Table 6.4: User-defined Settings	
Setting Name	Setting Description
$numSeeds$	Number of seeds that will be placed in the treatment area
$targetTumorExp$	Target radiation exposure for tumorous points in the treatment area

Dimensions

The dimensions relevant in this use case are the predefined points and the seeds to be placed in the treatment area, as shown in Table 6.5.

Table 6.5: Dimensions	
Dimension Name	Dimension Description
$p \in$ POINTS	Set of target points in the treatment area
$s \in$ SEEDS	Set of seeds to be placed in the treatment area

Data Parameters

Table 6.6 shows the coordinates for the predefined target points read from the INPUT_POINTS table.

Table 6.6: Data Parameters	
Parameter Name	Parameter Description
$pointX_p$	X coordinate for target point p
$pointY_p$	Y coordinate for target point p
$tumorFlg_p$	Flag indicating if point p has tumorous tissue

Decision Variables

The key decision variables are the exact locations (coordinates) for each seed, and an auxiliary variable that denotes the exposure for each point, as shown in Table 6.7.

Table 6.7: Decision Variables	
Variable Name	Variable Description
$SeedX_s$	X coordinate for seed s
$SeedY_s$	Y coordinate for seed s
$Exposure_p$	Radiation exposure at point p
$MaxExposure$	Maximum exposure across all p

Constraints

This use case imposes the following constraints:

$$\min_{p} pointX_p \leq SeedX_s \leq \max_{p} pointX_p \qquad \text{for all } s \qquad (6.1)$$

$$\min_{p} pointY_p \leq SeedY_s \leq \max_{p} pointY_p \qquad \text{for all } s \qquad (6.2)$$

$$Exposure_p =$$

$$\sum_{s} \frac{1}{\sqrt{(SeedX_s - pointX_p)^2 + (SeedY_s - pointY_p)^2 + 0.01}} \qquad \text{for all } p \qquad (6.3)$$

$$Exposure_p \geq targetTumorExp \qquad \text{for all}$$
$$p \,|\, tumorFlg_p = 1$$
$$(6.4)$$

$$MaxExposure \geq Exposure_p \qquad \text{for all } p \qquad (6.5)$$

Constraints (6.1) and (6.2) limit the placement of the seeds only to the treatment area as defined by the target points. Constraint (6.3) defines the total exposure at each point by calculating the Euclidean distance between each seed and each point and then applying the exposure equation we introduced earlier. We add a small perturbation value in the denominator to avoid division by zero. Constraint (6.4) requires the exposure on the tumorous tissue to be at least the target value. Finally, constraint (6.5), when modeled together with the objective function that minimizes the maximum exposure, sets the value of the $MaxExposure$ decision variable to the largest $Exposure_p$.

Objective Function

The objective in this use case is to minimize the maximum exposure for all target points:

$$\min \ MinMaxExposure = MaxExposure$$

6.2.4 Mathematical Formulation and SAS Model

Tables 6.8 and 6.9 show the mathematical formulation and the corresponding SAS code. The full code can be found in the supporting materials.

MATHEMATICS	SAS CODE
Table 6.8: SAS Code for Sets, Parameters, and Variables	
$numSeeds$	`num numSeeds;`
$targetTumorExp$	`num targetTumorExp;`
$p \in$ POINTS	`set POINTS;`
$s \in$ SEEDS	`set SEEDS = 1..numSeeds;`
$pointX_p$	`num pointX {POINTS};`
$pointY_p$	`num pointY {POINTS};`
$tumorFlg_p$	`num tumorFlg {POINTS};`
$SeedX_s$	`var SeedX {SEEDS};`
$SeedY_s$	`var SeedY {SEEDS};`
$Exposure_p$	`var Exposure {POINTS} >= 0;`
$MaxExposure$	`var MaxExposure >= 0;`

Table 6.9: SAS Code for Constraints and Objective Function

$\min_p pointX_p \leq SeedX_s \leq$ $\max_p pointX_p$ for all s	```con Xbounds {s in SEEDS}:``` ```min {p in POINTS} pointX[p] <= SeedX[s] <= max {p in POINTS} pointX[p];```
$\min_p pointY_p \leq SeedY_s \leq$ $\max_p pointY_p$ for all s	```con Ybounds {s in SEEDS}:``` ```min {p in POINTS} pointY[p] <= SeedY[s] <= max {p in POINTS} pointY[p];```

$Exposure_p$ for all p	```con ExposureDef {p in POINTS}:```
	```Exposure[p] =```
	```sum {s in SEEDS} (1 /```
	```(sqrt((SeedX[s] - pointX[p])^2 + (SeedY[s] - pointY[p])^2) + 0.01));```

$Exposure_p \geq$ $targetTumorExp$ for all $p\|tumorFlg_p = 1$	```con ExposureLowerBound {p in POINTS: tumorFlg[p] = 1}:``` ```Exposure[p] >= targetTumorExp;```
$MaxExposure \geq Exposure_p$ for all p	```con MaxExposureCon {p in POINTS}:``` ```MaxExposure >= Exposure[p];```
$\min MinMaxExposure = MaxExposure$	```min MinMaxExposure = MaxExposure;```

6.2.5   SAS Output

Figure 6.2 shows the Solution Summary produced by the SAS code, including the optimum value for the objective function.

The SAS System

The OPTMODEL Procedure

Solution Summary	
Solver	Multistart NLP
Algorithm	Interior Point Direct
Objective Function	MinMaxExposure
Solution Status	Optimal
Objective Value	3.000000907
Number of Starts	100
Number of Sample Points	3200
Number of Distinct Optima	79
Random Seed Used	6814260
Optimality Error	2.4924616E-8
Infeasibility	2.616183E-10
Presolve Time	0.00
Solution Time	0.29

Figure 6.2: SAS Output

6.2.6   Mathematical Formulation and Python Model

Tables 6.10 and 6.11 show the mathematical formulation and the corresponding Python code. The full code can be found in the supporting materials.

Table 6.10: Python Code for Sets, Parameters, and Variables	
MATHEMATICS	PYTHON CODE
$numSeeds$	`m.numSeeds=Param()`
$targetTumorExp$	`m.targetTumorExp=Param()`
$p \in \text{POINTS}$	`m.points = Set()`
$s \in \text{SEEDS}$	`m.seeds = RangeSet(1,m.numSeeds,1)`
$pointX_p$	`m.pointX = Param(m.points)`
$pointY_p$	`m.pointY = Param(m.points)`
$tumorFlg_p$	`m.tumorFlg = Param(m.points)`

$SeedX_s$ $SeedY_s$ $Exposure_p$ $MaxExposure$	`m.SeedX = Var(m.seeds, domain=Reals)`
	`m.SeedY = Var(m.seeds, domain=Reals)`
	`m.Exposure = Var(m.points,domain=NonNegativeReals)`
	`m.MaxExposure = Var(domain=NonNegativeReals)`

Table 6.11: Python Code for Constraints and Objective Function

Mathematical Formulation	Python Code

$\min_p pointX_p \leq SeedX_s \leq \max_p pointX_p$ for all s	```def Seed_Placement_X_Rule(m,s):```
	``` return (min(m.pointX[p] for p in m.points), m.SeedX[s],```
	``` max(m.pointX[p] for p in m.points))```
	```m.SeedPlacementXArea = Constraint(m.seeds,rule=Seed_Placement_X_Rule)```

$\min_p pointY_p \leq SeedY_s \leq \max_p pointY_p$ for all s	```def Seed_Placement_Y_Rule(m,s):```
	``` return (min(m.pointY[p] for p in m.points), m.SeedY[s],```
	``` max(m.pointY[p] for p in m.points))```
	```m.SeedPlacementYArea = Constraint(m.seeds,rule=Seed_Placement_Y_Rule)```

$Exposure_p$ for all p	```def Exposure_Def_Rule(m,p):```
	``` return sum(1/(((m.SeedX[s]-m.pointX[p])**(2)+```
	``` (m.SeedY[s]-m.pointY[p])**(2))**(1/2)+0.01) for s in m.seeds)```
	``` == m.Exposure[p]```
	```m.ExposureDefinition = Constraint(m.points,rule=Exposure_Def_Rule)```

$Exposure_p \geq targetTumorExp$ for all $p\|tumorFlg_p = 1$	```def Min_Tumor_Exp_Rule(m,p):```
	``` if m.tumorFlg[p]==1:```
	``` return m.Exposure[p] >= m.targetTumorExp```
	``` return Constraint.Skip```
	```m.MinTumorExposure = Constraint(m.points,rule=Min_Tumor_Exp_Rule)```

$MaxExposure \geq Exposure_p$ for all p	```def Max_Exposure_Rule(m,p):```
	``` return m.Exposure[p] <= m.MaxExposure```
	```m.MaxExposureRule = Constraint(m.points,rule=Max_Exposure_Rule)```

$\min MinMaxExposure = MaxExposure$	```def Min_Max_Exposure_Rule(m):```
	``` return (m.MaxExposure)```
	```m.MinMaxExposure= Objective(rule=Min_Max_Exposure_Rule, sense=minimize)```

6.2.7   Python Output

Figure 6.3 shows the output produced by the Python code, including the optimum value for the objective function.

```
Solver Status:

- Status: ok
  Message: Ipopt 3.11.1\x3a Optimal Solution Found
  Termination condition: optimal
  Id: 0
  Error rc: 0
  Time: 0.09293007850646973

Optimum Objective Function Value:

2.999999984664533
```

Figure 6.3: Python Output

6.2.8   Output Results

Table 6.12 shows a snapshot of the optimal results, representing the exact location (coordinates) where each seed should be placed. Figure 6.4 shows a heat map of the solution, with each of the three seed locations indicated by $*$ and the color representing the exposure. For example, the more red, the more the exposure for all seeds combined.

Table 6.12: Optimal Results Data Snapshot

Seed_ID	X_Coord	Y_Coord
1	2.5728	2.7079
2	3.6943	1.3182
3	1.3530	2.3167

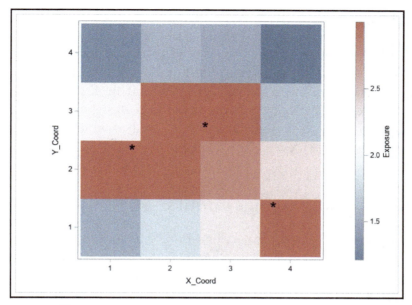

Figure 6.4: Heat Map of Optimal Exposure

6.3 Use Case: Optimizing Dike Heights for Flood Prevention

Flood prevention policies are relevant worldwide but even more critical in countries below sea level and high water levels, such as the Netherlands. The probability of a flood occurring can be extremely high, and consequences for human life can be disastrous. Several models have been proposed to select an optimum investment policy that specifies dikes, structures, and dunes construction characteristics while balancing investment and expected disaster management costs.

The following use case is derived and simplified from Brekelmans et al. [BHRE12], which won the 2013 Franz Edelman Award for Achievement in Advanced Analytics, Operations Research, and Management Science from INFORMS. The values of the parameters are extracted from a related publication by Eijgenraam et al. [EBdHR17].

6.3.1   Problem Definition

To address flood prevention, authorities need to decide how much to increment the height of existing dikes across a planning horizon. To balance investment and damage costs, nonlinear functions for estimating flood probability, construction cost, and investment cost are provided, all dependent on the height increase planned for each period, as well as several parameters estimated from historical data and provided in this problem.

6.3.2   Data and Settings Inputs

This application does not require explicit data but does require several parameters (or user-defined settings) that shape the nonlinear equations that define the flood probability, the investment costs, and the damage costs (user input). For code simplification, we will set these parameters directly in the formulation and code syntax instead of from a data input table as in previous applications.

6.3.3   Mathematical Formulation

User-defined Settings

Table 6.13 shows the user-defined settings that are considered constants in the mathematical model.

Table 6.13: User-defined Settings	
Setting Name	Setting Description
$prob0$	Initial flood probability
$damageCost0$	Initial damage cost
α	A shape parameter for the flood probability function
η	A shape parameter for the flood probability function
γ	Economic growth rate parameter
ζ	A shape parameter for the damage cost function
λ	A shape parameter for the investment cost function
c	A shape parameter for the investment cost function
b	A shape parameter for the investment cost function
$timeHorizon$	Number of periods in the planning horizon

Dimensions

The dimensions relevant in this use case are the periods in the planning horizon when decisions can be made, as shown in Table 6.14.

Table 6.14: Dimensions	
Dimension Name	Dimension Description
$p \in$ PERIODS	Set of periods in planning horizon

Decision Variables

The key decision variable is the height increment established for each period. Additional decision variables that support the formulation include the total height in each period, the flood probability associated with that height, and damage and investment costs, as shown in Table 6.15.

Table 6.15: Decision Variables	
Variable Name	Variable Description
$PeriodHeightInc_p$	Height increment for period p
$TotalHeightInc_p$	Cumulative height increment for period p
$FloodProb_p$	Probability of flood in period p
$DamageCost_p$	Damage cost due to flood in period p
$InvCost_p$	Investment cost for dike height increase in period p

Constraints

This use case imposes the following constraints:

$$TotalHeightInc_p = \sum_{p1=1}^{p} PeriodHeightInc_{p1} \qquad \text{for all } p \quad (6.6)$$

$$FloodProb_p = prob0 \times e^{\alpha(\eta p - TotalHeightInc_p)} \qquad \text{for all } p \quad (6.7)$$

$$DamageCost_p = damageCost0 \times e^{\gamma p + \zeta\, TotalHeightInc_p} \qquad \text{for all } p \quad (6.8)$$

$$InvCost_p = (c + bPeriodHeightInc_p) \times e^{\lambda\, TotalHeightInc_p} \quad \text{for all } p \quad (6.9)$$

Constraint (6.6) calculates the cumulative height increase by aggregating individual period increases. Constraint (6.7) defines the probability of a flood happening in period p, as a function of $TotalHeightInc_p$ and the given shape parameters. Similarly, constraints (6.8) and (6.9) define the damage and investment costs, respectively.

Objective Function

The objective in this use case is to minimize the total expected cost across all time periods:

$$\min\ TotalCost = \sum_p (FloodProb_p \times DamageCost_p + InvCost_p)$$

6.3.4 Mathematical Formulation and SAS Model

Tables 6.16 and 6.17 show the mathematical formulation and the corresponding SAS code. The full code can be found in the supporting materials.

Table 6.16: SAS Code for Sets, Parameters, and Variables

MATHEMATICS	SAS CODE
$prob0$	`num prob0 = 0.00044;`
$damageCost0$	`num damageCost0 = 1565;`
α	`num alpha = 0.0330;`
η	`num eta = 0.320;`
γ	`num gamma = 0.0196;`
ζ	`num zeta = 0.00377;`
λ	`num lambda = 0.0014;`
c	`num c = 16.69;`
b	`num b = 0.63;`
$timeHorizon$	`num timeHorizon = 100;`
$p \in \text{PERIODS}$	`set PERIODS = 1..timeHorizon;`
$PeriodHeightInc_p$	`var PeriodHeightInc {PERIODS} >= 0;`
$TotalHeightInc_p$	`var TotalHeightInc {PERIODS} >= 0;`
$FloodProb_p$	`var FloodProb {PERIODS} >= 0;`
$DamageCost_p$	`var DamageCost {PERIODS} >= 0;`
$InvCost_p$	`var InvCost {PERIODS} >= 0;`

Table 6.17: SAS Code for Constraints and Objective Function

$$TotalHeightInc_p = \sum_{p1=1}^{p} PeriodHeightInc_{p1} \text{ for all } p$$

$$FloodProb_p = prob0 \times e^{\alpha(\eta p - TotalHeightInc_p)} \text{ for all } p$$

$$DamageCost_p = damageCost0 \times e^{\gamma p + \zeta TotalHeightInc_p} \text{ for all } p$$

$$InvCost_p = (c + bPeriodHeightInc_p) \times e^{\lambda TotalHeightInc_p} \text{ for all } p$$

$$\min TotalCost = \sum_p (FloodProb_p \times DamageCost_p + InvCost_p)$$

```
con TotalHeightDef {p in PERIODS}:
   TotalHeightInc[p] = sum {p1 in PERIODS: p1 <= p} PeriodHeightInc[p1];

con FloodProbDef {p in PERIODS}:
   FloodProb[p] = prob0 * exp(alpha*(eta*p - TotalHeightInc[p]));

con DamageCostDef {p in PERIODS}:
   DamageCost[p] = damageCost0 * exp(gamma*p + zeta*TotalHeightInc[p]);

con InvCostDef {p in PERIODS}:
   InvCost[p] = (c + b*PeriodHeightInc[p]) * exp(lambda*TotalHeightInc[p]);

min TotalCost =
   sum {p in PERIODS} (FloodProb[p] * DamageCost[p] + InvCost[p]);
```

6.3.5   SAS Output

Figure 6.5 shows the Solution Summary produced by the SAS code, including the optimum value for the objective function.

The SAS System

The OPTMODEL Procedure

Solution Summary	
Solver	Multistart NLP
Algorithm	Interior Point Direct
Objective Function	TotalCost
Solution Status	Optimal
Objective Value	1910.229532
Number of Starts	59
Number of Sample Points	1600
Number of Distinct Optima	2
Random Seed Used	6064271
Optimality Error	9.126878E-12
Infeasibility	1.2699843E-7
Presolve Time	0.00
Solution Time	1.60

Figure 6.5: SAS Output

6.3.6   Mathematical Formulation and Python Model

Tables 6.18 and 6.19 show the mathematical formulation and the corresponding Python code. The full code can be found in the supporting materials.

Table 6.18: Python Code for Sets, Parameters, and Variables	
MATHEMATICS	PYTHON CODE
$prob0$	`m.prob0 = 0.00044`
$damageCost0$	`m.damageCost0 = 1565`
α	`m.alpha = 0.0330`
η	`m.eta = 0.320`
γ	`m.gamma = 0.0196`
ζ	`m.zeta = 0.00377`
λ	`m.lambda1 = 0.0014`
c	`m.c = 16.69;`
b	`m.b = 0.63;`
$timeHorizon$	`m.timeHorizon = 100`
$p \in$ PERIODS	`m.periods = RangeSet(1,m.timeHorizon,1)`
$PeriodHeightInc_p$	`m.PeriodHeightInc = Var(m.periods, domain=NonNegativeReals)`
$TotalHeightInc_p$	`m.TotalHeightInc = Var(m.periods, domain=NonNegativeReals)`
$FloodProb_p$	`m.FloodProb = Var(m.periods, domain=NonNegativeReals)`
$DamageCost_p$	`m.DamageCost = Var(m.periods, domain=NonNegativeReals)`
$InvCost_p$	`m.InvCost = Var(m.periods, domain=NonNegativeReals)`

Table 6.19: Python Code for Constraints and Objective Function

$$TotalHeightInc_p = \sum_{p1=1}^{p} PeriodHeightInc_{p1} \text{ for all } p$$

```python
def Total_H_Inc_Def_Rule(m,p):
    return (sum(m.PeriodHeightInc[p1] for p1 in m.periods if p1 <= p)
    == m.TotalHeightInc[p])
m.Total_H_Inc_Def = Constraint(m.periods,rule=Total_H_Inc_Def_Rule)
```

$$FloodProb_p = prob0 \times e^{\alpha(\eta p - TotalHeightInc_p)} \text{ for all } p$$

```python
def Flood_Prob_Def_Rule(m,p):
    return (m.prob0*exp(m.alpha*(m.eta*p-m.TotalHeightInc[p]))
    == m.FloodProb[p])
m.Flood_Prob_Def = Constraint(m.periods,rule=Flood_Prob_Def_Rule)
```

$$DamageCost_p = damageCost0 \times e^{\gamma p + \zeta TotalHeightInc_p} \text{ for all } p$$

```python
def Damage_Cost_Def_Rule(m,p):
    return (m.damageCost0*exp(m.gamma*p+m.zeta*m.TotalHeightInc[p])
    == m.DamageCost[p])
m.Damage_Cost_Def = Constraint(m.periods,rule=Damage_Cost_Def_Rule)
```

$$InvCost_p = (c + bPeriodHeightInc_p) \times e^{\lambda TotalHeightInc_p} \text{ for all } p$$

```python
def Inv_Cost_Def_Rule(m,p):
    return ((m.c+m.b*m.PeriodHeightInc[p])*
    exp(m.lambda1*(m.TotalHeightInc[p]))== m.InvCost[p])
m.Inv_Cost_Def = Constraint(m.periods,rule=Inv_Cost_Def_Rule)
```

$$\min TotalCost = \sum_p (FloodProb_p \times DamageCost_p + InvCost_p)$$

```python
def Min_Total_Cost_Rule(m):
    return (sum(m.FloodProb[p]*m.DamageCost[p]+m.InvCost[p]
    for p in m.periods))
m.Min_Total_Cost = Objective(rule=Min_Total_Cost_Rule, sense=minimize)
```

6.3.7   Python Output

Figure 6.6 shows the output produced by the Python code, including the optimum value for the objective function.

```
Solver Status:

- Status: ok
  Message: Ipopt 3.11.1\x3a Optimal Solution Found
  Termination condition: optimal
  Id: 0
  Error rc: 0
  Time: 0.1491379737854004

Optimum Objective Function Value:
1910.2295282458997
```

Figure 6.6: Python Output

6.3.8   Output Results

Table 6.20 shows a snapshot of the optimal results that represent the height increase to be added during each period.

Table 6.20: Optimal Results Data Snapshot

Period	Height_Increase
1	0.00004
2	0.00005
3	0.00009
4	0.00068
5	0.44299
6	0.75764

Figure 6.7 shows a plot of the optimal solution, together with the resulting flood probabilities. As expected, flood probabilities decrease with the increase in height.

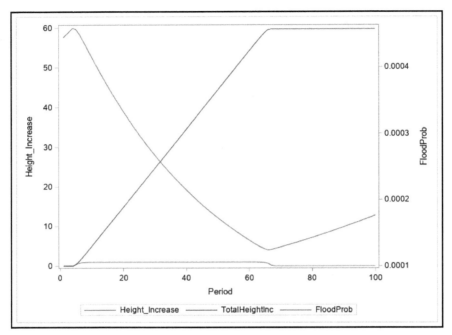

Figure 6.7: Optimal Solution and Flood Probabilities

6.4   Practice Problems

1. A thrift store needs to create a markdown plan for ten items to make space
   for newer seasonal items that they expect to be donated over the next two
   weeks. The current price of each item (dollars per pound) and current
   inventory (in pounds) are provided in NLP_P2_item_base_prices.csv. The
   store cannot hold more than 15 pounds of these items by the end of the
   planning horizon. Any inventory left at the end of the horizon will need to
   be disposed at the store's expense of $1.2 per pound. Assume the following
   simplified price-demand relationship for each product p:

   $$Demand_p = \frac{BasePrice_p - MarkedPrice_p}{BasePrice_p} \times Inventory_p$$

   Build an optimum pricing plan for each item to maximize the store's revenue (accounting for the items' disposal). What is the optimum revenue
   by the end of the planning horizon?

2. For the Seed Placement use case, omit constraints (6.1) and (6.2), and instead impose lower and upper bounds on the $SeedX_s$ and $SeedY_s$ variables. In SAS, you can do this in the VAR statement or by modifying the .lb and .ub variable suffixes. Compare the presolved problem statistics from the log before and after this change.

3. For the Seed Placement use case, solve the problem with the number of seeds changed to 1, 2, and 4, and compare the resulting solutions.

4. For the Seed Placement use case, modify the code to instead minimize the total exposure $\sum_p Exposure_p$ subject to $Exposure_p \geq targetTumorExp$ for all tumorous p.

5. For the Flood Prevention use case, modify the code to disallow height increases for the first 50, 75, and 100 years and investigate the resulting optimal solutions.

6. For the Flood Prevention use case, modify the input parameters to increase damage cost and/or decrease investment cost and describe the effect on the optimal solution.

Chapter 7

Network Optimization

Networks are often used to model optimization problems that involve relationships between pairs of entities. This chapter first reviews network optimization concepts and then presents two use cases based on real applications, followed by several practice problems related to these use cases.

7.1 Concepts Review

A network consists of a set of objects called *nodes* and a set of *links*, which represent relationships between pairs of nodes. For example, in a road network, the nodes correspond to intersections, a link between two nodes corresponds to a road that joins them, and a common optimization problem is to find a shortest path between two specified nodes in the network. One approach to solve a network optimization problem is to explicitly introduce decision variables, a linear objective, and linear constraints and then call either a linear programming solver or a mixed integer linear programming solver. SAS also provides a network solver that invokes specialized algorithms to solve several classes of network problems, including:

- biconnected components
- clique enumeration
- connected components
- cycle enumeration
- linear assignment
- maximum flow
- minimum-cost network flow

93

- minimum cut
- minimum spanning tree
- path enumeration
- shortest paths
- topological sort
- transitive closure
- traveling salesman problem
- vehicle routing problem

For these problems, you need only specify the nodes, links, and any relevant numeric attributes (such as link weights), rather than explicitly defining variables, objective, and constraints. For more information about the network solver in SAS, see the network solver chapter in [SAS23].

The use cases in this chapter correspond to the traveling salesman problem (TSP) and the vehicle routing problem (VRP). In the TSP, you are given a set of nodes and a set of links, and each link has a weight that represents the distance between those two nodes. The problem is to find an optimal *tour* that visits each node exactly once and minimizes the total distance traveled as measured by the sum of the link weights. The idea for the colorful name of this problem is that the nodes represent cities and the tour represents the travel itinerary of a salesman who leaves his home city, visits each other city, and returns home. Figure 7.1 shows an optimal TSP solution for a complete network with 200 nodes, where each link weight is the Euclidean distance between the two nodes.

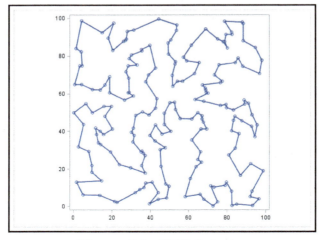

Figure 7.1: TSP Solution

In the VRP, one node represents a depot, and the other nodes represent customers, each with a demand that must be satisfied. Each link weight again corresponds to travel distance (or cost). You are also given a set of vehicles, each of which has a capacity that limits the total demand it can serve. The problem is to find an optimal set of subtours (one per vehicle) that start and end at the depot and together visit each customer exactly once, while respecting the vehicle capacities and minimizing the total cost as measured by the sum of the link weights across all vehicles. Figure 7.2 shows an optimal VRP solution for a complete network with 21 customers (22 nodes), where the node labels are the customer demands, each vehicle has a capacity of 3000, and the link weights are Euclidean distances.

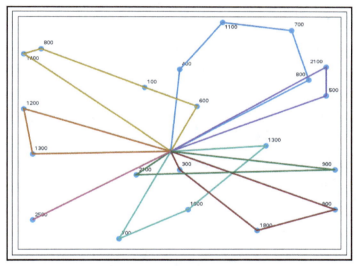

Figure 7.2: VRP Solution

For in-depth information about network models and solution algorithms, please refer to [Ber91].

7.2   Use Case: Optimizing Clinical Samples Routing in Malawi—TSP

Access to diagnostic testing services is a critical element of public health systems in countries with high prevalence of communicable diseases such as HIV and tuberculosis. These testing services require daily logistics collecting and transporting clinical samples for their processing. Efficient routes are key to a timely delivery of samples and patient diagnosis.

In this section we will review a simplified version of daily route optimization work performed by Gibson et al. [GDJ+23] that won the "Doing Good with Good OR" prize from INFORMS in 2020. This simplification is modeled as a Traveling Salesman Problem (TSP) to find a route where a set of locations has to be visited exactly once, minimizing the overall travel distance. See [ABCC06] for a comprehensive description of state-of-the-art approaches to solving the TSP. We will use a simple (but less efficient) compact formulation that was proposed by Miller, Tucker, and Zemlin in [MTZ60].

7.2.1   Problem Definition

Several locations have lab samples that need to be picked up and delivered to the lab for processing. We assume there is only one vehicle that leaves the lab and comes back to the lab after visiting all the locations.

7.2.2   Data and Settings Inputs

This model requires distances between all locations (data input).

The data dictionary in Table 7.1 contains more detailed information about the table and the variables.

Table 7.1: Data Dictionary			
Data Table	Variable Name	Variable Type	Variable Description
INPUT_DIST	From	Num	Facility from which vehicle is leaving (e.g., 1)
INPUT_DIST	To	Num	Facility to which vehicle is traveling (e.g., 2)
INPUT_DIST	Dist	Num	Distance (e.g., 4.3)

Table 7.2 shows a snapshot of the input data.

Table 7.2: INPUT_DIST Data Snapshot

From	To	Dist
1	2	7.27
1	3	3.58
1	4	3.04

7.2.3   Mathematical Formulation

Dimensions

For standardization with the TSP literature, we will refer to locations as *nodes* and connections between pairs of nodes as *links*. The dimensions relevant in this use case are the sets of nodes and links, as shown in Table 7.3.

Table 7.3: Dimensions	
Dimension Name	Dimension Description
$i \in$ NODES	Set of locations
$(i,j) \in$ LINKS	Set of connections between a pair of nodes

Data Parameters

Table 7.4 shows the input parameters read from the INPUT_DIST table.

Table 7.4: Data Parameters	
Parameter Name	Parameter Description
N	Number of nodes to visit
$dist_{i,j}$	Distance from node i to node j

Decision Variables

The key decision variables are whether link (i,j) is used and in what order node i is visited, as shown in Table 7.5.

Table 7.5: Decision Variables

Variable Name	Variable Description
$Use_{i,j}$	Binary variable to indicate whether link (i,j) is used in the vehicle route
$Order_i$	Order of visiting nodes

Constraints

This use case imposes the following constraints:

$$\sum_{i \neq j} Use_{i,j} = 1 \qquad \text{for all } j \qquad (7.1)$$

$$\sum_{j \neq i} Use_{i,j} = 1 \qquad \text{for all } i \qquad (7.2)$$

$$Order_i - Order_j + N \times Use_{i,j} \leq N - 1 \qquad \text{for all } (i,j) \mid j \neq 1 \qquad (7.3)$$

Constraints (7.1) and (7.2) require that each node is visited and left exactly once. Constraint (7.3) guarantees that there are no subtours; that is, the route is one large tour. For simplicity, we assume that the lab is node 1. To see that (7.3) eliminates subtours, suppose C is the set of links in a (nonempty) subtour that does not contain node 1. Then adding up (7.3) along the subtour would yield

$$\sum_{(i,j) \in C} (Order_i - Order_j + N \times 1) \leq \sum_{(i,j) \in C} (N-1),$$

which simplifies to the false statement

$$N|C| \leq (N-1)|C|,$$

so any solution that contains such a subtour would violate the constraints.

Objective Function

The objective in this use case is to minimize travel distance:

$$\min \ TotalCost = \sum_{i,j} dist_{i,j} \times Use_{i,j}$$

7.2.4 Mathematical Formulation and SAS Model

Tables 7.6 and 7.7 show the mathematical formulation and the corresponding SAS code. The full code can be found in the supporting materials.

Table 7.6: SAS Code for Sets, Parameters, and Variables	
MATHEMATICS	SAS CODE
N	`num n = card(NODES);`
$(i, j) \in$ LINKS $i \in$ NODES	`set <num,num> LINKS;` `set NODES = union {<i,j> in LINKS} {i,j};`
$dist_{i,j}$	`num dist {LINKS};`
$Use_{i,j}$ $Order_i$	`var Use {LINKS} binary;` `var Order {NODES} >= 0 <= n - 1 integer;`

Table 7.7: SAS Code for Constraints and Objective Function	
$\sum_{i \neq j} Use_{i,j} = 1$ for all j	`con EnterNode {j in NODES}:` `  sum {<i,(j)> in LINKS} Use[i,j] = 1;`
$\sum_{j \neq i} Use_{i,j} = 1$ for all i	`con LeaveNode {i in NODES}:` `  sum {<(i),j> in LINKS} Use[i,j] = 1;`
$Order_i - Order_j + N \times Use_{i,j} \leq$ $N - 1$ for all $(i,j) \mid j \neq 1$	`con NoSubtours {<i,j> in LINKS: j ne 1}:` `  Order[i] + 1 - Order[j] <= n * (1 - Use[i,j]);`
min $TotalCost =$ $\sum_{i,j} dist_{i,j} \times Use_{i,j}$	`min TotalCost =` `  sum {<i,j> in LINKS} dist[i,j] * Use[i,j];`

7.2.5 SAS Output

Figure 7.3 shows the Solution Summary produced by the SAS code, including the optimum value for the objective function. A more detailed sample output is presented in section 7.2.8.

The SAS System	
The OPTMODEL Procedure	
Solution Summary	
Solver	MILP
Algorithm	Branch and Cut
Objective Function	TotalCost
Solution Status	Optimal
Objective Value	25.92
Relative Gap	0
Absolute Gap	0
Primal Infeasibility	0
Bound Infeasibility	0
Integer Infeasibility	0
Best Bound	25.92
Nodes	1
Solutions Found	1
Iterations	30
Presolve Time	0.12
Solution Time	0.13

Figure 7.3: SAS Output

7.2.6 Mathematical Formulation and Python Model

Tables 7.8 and 7.9 show the mathematical formulation and the corresponding Python code. Please notice in this specific case, for the Python code to run properly, the N parameter needs to be defined before the NODES set and the *dist* parameter needs to be defined after the LINKS set. The full code can be found in the supporting materials.

Table 7.8: Python Code for Sets, Parameters, and Variables

MATHEMATICS	PYTHON CODE
N	```m.N = len(pd.unique(input_dist['From']))```

$i \in$ NODES
 	
 $(i,j) \in$ LINKS
	```m.nodes = RangeSet(1,m.N)```
	
	 ```m.links = Set(initialize=[(i,j)```
	``` for i in m.nodes for j in m.nodes if i != j])```

$dist_{i,j}$	```m.dist = Param(m.links)```

$Use_{i,j}$
 	
 $Order_i$
	```m.Use = Var(m.links, domain=Binary)```
	
	 ```m.Order = Var(m.nodes, domain=NonNegativeIntegers,```
	``` bounds=(0,m.N-1))```

Table 7.9: Python Code for Constraints and Objective Function

MATHEMATICS	PYTHON CODE

$\sum_{i \neq j} Use_{i,j} = 1$
 for all j
	```def Enter_Once_Rule(m,j):```
	``` return (sum(m.Use[i,j] for i in m.nodes if i!=j) == 1)```
	```m.Enter_All = Constraint(m.nodes,rule=Enter_Once_Rule)```

$\sum_{j \neq i} Use_{i,j} = 1$
 for all i
	```def Leave_Once_Rule(m,i):```
	``` return (sum(m.Use[i,j] for j in m.nodes if i!=j) == 1)```
	```m.Leave_All = Constraint(m.nodes,rule=Leave_Once_Rule)```

$Order_i - Order_j + N \times$
 $Use_{i,j} \leq$
 $N-1$ for all $(i,j) \mid j \neq 1$
	```def NoSubT_Rule(m,i,j):```
	``` if j!=1: return (m.Order[i] - m.Order[j]```
	``` + m.N * m.Use[i,j] <= m.N-1)```
	``` else: return Constraint.Skip```
	```m.NoSubT = Constraint(m.links, rule=NoSubT_Rule)```

min $TotalCost =$
 $\sum_{i,j} dist_{i,j} \times Use_{i,j}$
	```def Min_Cost_Rule(m):```
	``` return (sum(m.dist[i,j]*m.Use[i,j] for i,j in m.links))```
	```m.Min_Cost = Objective(rule=Min_Cost_Rule,```
	```sense=minimize)```

7.2.7   Python Output

Figure 7.4 shows the output produced by the Python code, including the optimum value for the objective function. A more detailed sample output is presented in section 7.2.8.

```
Solver Status:

- Status: ok
  Termination condition: optimal
  Statistics:
    Branch and bound:
      Number of bounded subproblems: 1
      Number of created subproblems: 1
  Error rc: 0
  Time: 0.04198598861694336

Optimum Objective Function Value:
25.92
```

Figure 7.4: Python Output

7.2.8   Output Results

Table 7.10 shows a snapshot of optimal results. This is the set of links that are part of the optimal route.

Table 7.10: Optimal Results Data Snapshot

From	To
1	4
4	5
5	8

7.3   Use Case: Optimizing Clinical Samples Routing in Malawi—VRP

Building on the previous section's use case, we are now going to expand the Traveling Salesman Problem (TSP) to a Vehicle Routing Problem (VRP). The main differentiation is the ability of a VRP to model several routes with capacitated vehicles.

7.3.1   Problem Definition

This expansion to VRP enables us to model this clinical samples routing problem more realistically by introducing demand for each location as well as a capacity for each vehicle.

7.3.2   Data and Settings Inputs

This application requires distances between all pairs of locations as well as demand for each location (data input).

The data dictionary in Table 7.11 contains more detailed information about the tables and the variables.

Table 7.11: Data Dictionary			
Data Table	Variable Name	Variable Type	Variable Description
INPUT_DIST	From	Num	Facility from which vehicle is leaving (e.g., 1)
INPUT_DIST	To	Num	Facility to which vehicle is traveling (e.g., 2)
INPUT_DIST	Dist	Num	Distance (e.g., 4.3)
INPUT_DEMAND	Location	Num	Facility numeric identification (e.g., 1)
INPUT_DEMAND	Demand	Num	Number of samples required to be picked up (e.g., 5)

Tables 7.12 and 7.13 show a snapshot of the input data.

Table 7.12: INPUT_DIST Data Snapshot

From	To	Dist
1	2	7.27
1	3	3.58
1	4	3.04

Table 7.13: INPUT_DEMAND Data Snapshot

Location	Demand
1	0
2	5
3	7

7.3.3 Mathematical Formulation

User-defined Settings

Table 7.14 shows the user-defined settings. For simplicity, we assume that each vehicle has the same capacity.

Table 7.14: User-defined Settings	
Setting Name	Setting Description
numVehicles	Total number of available vehicles
cap	Vehicle capacity (assuming that all vehicles have the same capacity)

Dimensions

For standardization with the VRP literature, we will refer to locations as *nodes* and connections between pairs of nodes as *links*. The dimensions relevant in this use case are the sets of nodes and links, as shown in Table 7.15.

Table 7.15: Dimensions	
Dimension Name	Dimension Description
$i \in$ NODES	Set of locations
$(i, j) \in$ LINKS	Set of connections between a pair of nodes

Data Parameters

Table 7.16 shows the input parameters read from the INPUT_DIST and INPUT_DEMAND tables.

Table 7.16: Data Parameters	
Parameter Name	Parameter Description
N	Number of nodes to visit
$dist_{i,j}$	Distance from node i to node j
dem_i	Demand at node i

Decision Variables

The key decision variables are whether link (i, j) is used and the cumulative demand after visiting node i, as shown in Table 7.17.

Table 7.17: Decision Variables	
Variable Name	Variable Description
$Use_{i,j}$	Binary variable to indicate whether link (i, j) is used in the vehicle route
$CDem_i$	Cumulative demand after visiting node i

Constraints

This use case imposes the following constraints:

$$\sum_{i \neq j} Use_{i,j} = 1 \qquad \text{for all } j \neq 1 \quad (7.4)$$

$$\sum_{j \neq i} Use_{i,j} = 1 \qquad \text{for all } i \neq 1 \quad (7.5)$$

$$\sum_{i \neq 1} Use_{i,1} = numVehicles \qquad (7.6)$$

$$\sum_{j \neq 1} Use_{1,j} = numVehicles \qquad (7.7)$$

$$CDem_i + dem_j - CDem_j \leq (cap + dem_j) \times (1 - Use_{i,j}) \qquad \text{for all } (i, j) \mid j \neq 1 \quad (7.8)$$

$$CDem_j - CDem_i - dem_j \leq (cap - dem_j) \times (1 - Use_{i,j}) \qquad \text{for all } (i, j) \mid j \neq 1 \quad (7.9)$$

Constraints (7.4) and (7.5) require that each node other than the lab is visited and left exactly once. For simplicity, we assume that the lab is node 1. Constraints (7.6) and (7.7) require that the lab is visited and left exactly *numVehicles* times (once per vehicle). Constraint (7.8) guarantees that each vehicle's route consists of a single subtour. Constraint (7.9) is not required but yields more interpretable output by preventing $CDem_j$ from overestimating the actual cumulative demand at node j.

Objective Function

The objective in this use case is to minimize travel distance:

$$\min\ TotalCost = \sum_{i,j} dist_{i,j} \times Use_{i,j}$$

7.3.4   Mathematical Formulation and SAS Model

Tables 7.18 and 7.19 show the mathematical formulation and the corresponding SAS code. The full code can be found in the supporting materials.

Table 7.18: SAS Code for Sets, Parameters, and Variables	
MATHEMATICS	SAS CODE
$numVehicles$	`num numVehicles = 3;`
cap	`num cap = 100;`
N	`num n = card(NODES);`
$(i,j) \in$ LINKS	`set <num,num> LINKS;`
$i \in$ NODES	`set NODES = union {<i,j> in LINKS} {i,j};`
$dist_{i,j}$	`num dist {LINKS};`
dem_i	`num dem {NODES};`
$Use_{i,j}$	`var Use {LINKS} binary;`
$CDem_i$	`var CDem {NODES} >= 0 <= cap;`

Table 7.19: SAS Code for Constraints and Objective Function

Mathematical notation	SAS code
$\sum_{i\neq j} Use_{i,j} = 1$ for all $j \neq 1$	`con EnterNode {j in NODES diff {1}}:` `sum {<i,(j)> in LINKS} Use[i,j] = 1;`
$\sum_{i\neq j} Use_{i,j} = 1$ for all $i \neq 1$	`con LeaveNode {i in NODES diff {1}}:` `sum {<(i),j> in LINKS} Use[i,j] = 1;`
$\sum_{i\neq 1} Use_{i,1} = numVehicles$	`con EnterDepot:` `sum {<i,1> in LINKS} Use[i,1] = numVehicles;`
$\sum_{j\neq 1} Use_{1,j} = numVehicles$	`con LeaveDepot:` `sum {<1,j> in LINKS} Use[1,j] = numVehicles;`

$CDem_i + dem_j - CDem_j \leq (cap + dem_j) \times (1 - Use_{i,j})$ for all $(i,j) \mid j \neq 1$	`con NoSubtours {<i,j> in LINKS: j ne 1}:`
	`CDem[i] + dem[j] - CDem[j] <=`
	`(CDem[i].ub + dem[j] - CDem[j].lb) * (1 - Use[i,j]);`

$CDem_j - CDem_i - dem_j \leq (cap - dem_j) \times (1 - Use_{i,j})$ for all $(i,j) \mid j \neq 1$	`con NoSubtours2 {<i,j> in LINKS: j ne 1}:`
	`CDem[j] - CDem[i] - dem[j] <=`
	`(CDem[j].ub - CDem[i].lb - dem[j]) * (1 - Use[i,j]);`

min $TotalCost = \sum_{i,j} dist_{i,j} \times Use_{i,j}$	`min TotalCost =` `sum {<i,j> in LINKS} dist[i,j] * Use[i,j];`

7.3.5   SAS Output

Figure 7.5 shows the Solution Summary produced by the SAS code, including the optimum value for the objective function. A more detailed sample output is presented in section 7.3.8.

The SAS System

The OPTMODEL Procedure

Solution Summary	
Solver	Network
Problem Type	Vehicle Routing
Solution Status	Optimal
Objective Value	39.95
Relative Gap	0
Absolute Gap	0
Primal Infeasibility	0
Bound Infeasibility	0
Integer Infeasibility	0
Best Bound	39.95
Nodes	1
Iterations	23
Solution Time	0.03

Figure 7.5: SAS Output

7.3.6   Mathematical Formulation and Python Model

Tables 7.20 and 7.21 show the mathematical formulation and the corresponding Python code. Please notice in this specific case, for the Python code to run properly, the N parameter needs to be defined before the NODES set and the *dist* parameter needs to be defined after the LINKS set. The full code can be found in the supporting materials.

Table 7.20: Python Code for Sets, Parameters, and Variables	
MATHEMATICS	PYTHON CODE
numVehicles	`m.numVehicles = 3`
cap	`m.cap = 100`
N	`m.N = len(pd.unique(input_dist['From']))`
$i \in$ NODES	`m.nodes = RangeSet(1,m.N)`
$(i,j) \in$ LINKS	`m.links = Set(initialize=[(i,j)` `  for i in m.nodes for j in m.nodes if i != j])`
$dist_{i,j}$	`m.dist = Param(m.links)`
dem_i	`m.dem = Param(m.nodes)`
$Use_{i,j}$	`m.Use = Var(m.links, domain=Binary)`
$CDem_i$	`m.CDem= Var(m.nodes, bounds=(0,m.cap))`

Table 7.21: Python Code for Constraints and Objective Function

$$\sum_{i\neq j} Use_{i,j} = 1 \quad \text{for all } j \neq 1$$

```python
def Enter_Node_Rule(m,j):
    return (sum(m.Use[i,j] for i in m.nodes if i!=j) == 1)
m.Enter_Node = Constraint(m.nodes,rule=Enter_Node_Rule)
```

$$\sum_{i\neq j} Use_{i,j} = 1 \quad \text{for all } i \neq 1$$

```python
def Leave_Node_Rule(m,i):
    return (sum(m.Use[i,j] for j in m.nodes if i!=j) == 1)
m.Leave_Node = Constraint(m.nodes,rule=Leave_Node_Rule)
```

$$\sum_{i\neq 1} Use_{i,1} = numVehicles$$

```python
def Enter_Depo_Rule(m):
    return (sum(m.Use[i,j] for i in m.nodes if i!=j) == 1)
m.Enter_Depo = Constraint(m.nodes,rule=Enter_Depo_Rule)
```

$$\sum_{j\neq 1} Use_{1,j} = numVehicles$$

```python
def Leave_Depo_Rule(m):
    return (sum(m.Use[i,j] for j in m.nodes if i!=j) == 1)
m.Leave_Depo = Constraint(m.nodes,rule=Leave_Depo_Rule)
```

$$CDem_i + dem_j - CDem_j \leq (cap + dem_j) \times (1 - Use_{i,j}) \text{ for all } (i,j) \mid j \neq 1$$

```python
def No_SubTour1_Rule(m,i,j):
    if j!=1: return (m.CDem[i] + m.dem[j] - m.CDem[j] <=
(m.cap + m.dem[j])*(1 - m.Use[i,j]))
    else: return Constraint.Skip
m.No_SubTour1 = Constraint(m.links, rule=No_SubTour1_Rule)
```

$$CDem_j - CDem_i - dem_j \leq (cap - dem_j) \times (1 - Use_{i,j}) \text{ for all } (i,j) \mid j \neq 1$$

```python
def No_SubTour2_Rule(m,i,j):
    if j!=1: return (m.CDem[j] - m.CDem[i] - m.dem[j] <=
(m.cap - m.dem[j])*(1 - m.Use[i,j]))
    else: return Constraint.Skip
m.No_SubTour2 = Constraint(m.links, rule=No_SubTour2_Rule)
```

$$\min TotalCost = \sum_{i,j} dist_{i,j} \times Use_{i,j}$$

```python
def Min_Cost_Rule(m):
    return (sum(m.dist[i,j]*m.Use[i,j] for i,j in m.links))
m.Min_Cost = Objective(rule=Min_Cost_Rule,
sense=minimize)
```

7.3.7 Python Output

Figure 7.6 shows the output produced by the Python code, including the optimum value for the objective function. A more detailed sample output is presented in section 7.3.8.

```
Solver Status:

- Status: ok
  Termination condition: optimal
  Statistics:
    Branch and bound:
      Number of bounded subproblems: 1
      Number of created subproblems: 1
  Error rc: 0
  Time: 0.036968231201171875

Optimum Objective Function Value:
39.95
```

Figure 7.6: Python Output

7.3.8 Output Results

Table 7.22 shows a snapshot of optimal results. This is the set of links that are part of the optimal route.

Table 7.22: Optimal Results Data Snapshot

From	To
1	4
4	1
1	5
5	8

7.4 Practice Problems

1. A Food Bank organization needs to assign existing distribution depots to three regions. The weekly fixed cost for transporting food from each depot

to each region is provided in Table 7.23. Each region needs to have exactly one depot assigned. What is the optimum assignment of depots to regions?

Table 7.23: Data for problem 1

From/To	Region 1	Region 2	Region 3
NY	25	45	55
NJ	52	19	30
PA	29	38	21
CT	18	54	39

2. For the TSP use case, omit the subtour elimination constraint (7.3) and investigate the resulting solution.
3. For the TSP use case, replace the subtour elimination constraint (7.3) with an indicator constraint in SAS as follows:
   ```
   con NoSubtours {<i,j> in LINKS: j ne 1}:
      Use[i,j] = 1 implies Order[i] + 1 <= Order[j];
   ```

4. For the TSP use case, strengthen the subtour elimination constraint (7.3) as follows:

$$Order_i - Order_j + N \times Use_{i,j} + (N - 2) \times Use_{j,i} \leq N - 1$$

Compare the initial linear programming bound before and after this change.
5. For the TSP use case, call the network solver in SAS by executing the following statements:
   ```
   set <num,num> TOUR;
   solve with network /
      tsp direction=directed include=(weight=dist) out=(tour=TOUR);
   put TOUR=;
   ```
6. For the VRP use case, investigate the effect of increasing and decreasing the number of vehicles by 1.
7. For the VRP use case, omit constraint (7.9) and investigate the effect on the resulting *CDem* values. Does the optimal objective value change?
8. For the VRP use case, replace constraints (7.8) and (7.9) with an indicator constraint in SAS as follows:
   ```
   con NoSubtours {<i,j> in LINKS: j ne 1}:
      Use[i,j] = 1 implies CDem[i] + dem[j] = CDem[j];
   ```

9. For the VRP use case, call the network solver in SAS by executing the following statements:

```
set DEPOT = {1};
set <num,num,num,num> VRPLINKS; /* route, order, from, to */
solve with network /
    vrp=(depot=DEPOT capacity=(cap) demand=dem
        minRoutes=(numVehicles) maxRoutes=(numVehicles))
    direction=directed include=(weight=dist)
    out=(vrplinks=VRPLINKS);
put VRPLINKS=;
```

Chapter 8

Multicriteria Optimization

Optimization problems often involve multiple, sometimes competing, objectives. This chapter first reviews multicriteria optimization concepts and then presents a use case based on a real application, followed by several practice problems related to this use case.

8.1   Concepts Review

Pareto Frontier

For an optimization problem with a single objective, comparing two feasible solutions is often straightforward: the solution with the better objective value is preferred. For an optimization problem with multiple objectives, however, the situation is more complicated. For example, suppose there are two objectives. If solution A has better values than solution B for both objectives, then solution A is preferred, and solution B is said to be *dominated* by solution A. But if solution A is better than solution B for one objective and worse than solution B for the other objective, the decision maker needs to evaluate the trade-off to decide between these two solutions. These two solutions are then called *nondominated*, and the set of all nondominated solutions is called the *Pareto frontier*.

Some solvers, including the black-box optimization solver in SAS, naturally handle multiple objectives and return a set of nondominated solutions that approximate the Pareto frontier. The decision maker can then select one of these solutions, perhaps based on additional considerations that are not captured in the optimization model. For more information about the black-box optimization solver in SAS, see the black-box optimization solver chapter in [SAS23].

Blended Objective

Many optimization solvers optimize only one objective function at a time. A common way to handle multiple objectives is to blend them into a single objective with nonnegative weights that reflect the relative importance of each objective. Explicitly, if there are k objective functions $f_1, \ldots, f_k$ to be minimized, you would specify nonnegative weights α_i for $i \in \{1, \ldots, k\}$ and minimize the blended objective function $\sum_{i=1}^{k} \alpha_i f_i$. With this approach, it is important to consider the magnitudes of the various objective functions, especially if they are measured in different units, so that one objective does not completely drown out the effect of the others.

Sequential Algorithm

The most commonly used algorithm in practice for multicriteria optimization is the *sequential* (also called *lexicographic*) approach. It does require two additional but typically intuitive inputs: prioritization of the objective functions and a tolerance associated with each objective function. This algorithm then optimizes one objective function at a time in order of the given prioritization, adding a cut after each solve, not allowing previous objective function(s) to degrade more than the associated tolerance.

For in-depth information about multicriteria optimization models and solution algorithms, please refer to [Ehr05].

8.2 Use Case: Optimizing the San Francisco Police Patrol Schedule

In 1988, the San Francisco Police Department (SFPD) performed a first-of-its-kind approach to police officer patrol scheduling [TH89], which earned them the 1988 Franz Edelman Award for Achievement in Advanced Analytics, Operations Research, and Management Science from INFORMS.

Like most police departments, SFPD needs to build daily schedules for police patrols, accounting for several relevant metrics such as citizen safety, cost of operations, and officers call time, among others. Police departments build estimates of the required number of police officers for different locations at different times of day and days of the week. Efficient schedules require balancing the workload by minimizing shortages (not enough police officers) as well as surpluses (too many police officers).

8.2.1 Problem Definition

To formulate this scheduling problem with an optimization model, we define decision variables as the number of patrol officers scheduled to begin their shifts at each time of day. This is a widely used approach that enables a more compact formulation than deciding how many officers are patrolling at each time of day. To produce a reasonable schedule, we need to minimize shortages while not scheduling more officers than are available. However, there are several meaningful ways to measure shortage, each measure translating into a different citizen safety concern. The total shortage (calculated as a sum of all unmet needs across all time windows) measures the overall safety concern, whereas the maximum shortage (calculated as the maximum unmet need across all time windows) measures the largest safety concern over time.

8.2.2 Data and Settings Inputs

This application requires an estimate of the required number of officers for each time window (data input).

The data dictionary in Table 8.1 contains more detailed information about the table and the variables.

Table 8.1: Data Dictionary			
Data Table	Variable Name	Variable Type	Variable Description
INPUT_DEMAND	Time	Num	Beginning hour of the time window (e.g., 2)
INPUT_DEMAND	Demand	Num	Estimate of required number of officers patrolling (e.g., 2)
INPUT_SETTINGS	Setting_Name	Char	Name of the configuration setting (e.g., CAPACITY)
INPUT_SETTINGS	Setting_Value	Num	Value of the configuration setting (e.g., 40)
INPUT_SETTINGS	Setting_Desc	Char	Description of the configuration setting

Table 8.2 shows a snapshot of the input data.

Table 8.2: INPUT_DEMAND Data Snapshot

Time	Demand
0	19
1	7
2	6

8.2.3   Mathematical Formulation

User-defined Settings

Table 8.3 shows the user-defined settings that are considered constant in the mathematical model. Please notice that *tolerance* is also provided as part of the required inputs to use the Sequential Algorithm.

Table 8.3: User-defined Settings	
Setting Name	Setting Description
capacity	Total number of available patrol officers
duration	Number of hours in a work shift
tolerance	Amount by which to relax primary objective when optimizing secondary objective

Dimensions

The dimensions relevant in this use case are the overall set of times and the times in a given shift, as shown in Table 8.4.

Table 8.4: Dimensions	
Dimension Name	Dimension Description
$t \in$ TIMES	Set of times (one per hour)
$t \in$ TIMES$_s$	Set of times in shift s

Data Parameters

Table 8.5 shows the input parameter read from the INPUT_DEMAND table.

Table 8.5: Data Parameter	
Parameter Name	Parameter Description
$demand_t$	Demand for patrolling officers at time t

Decision Variables

The key decision variable is the number of officers who start their shifts at time t, as shown in Table 8.6. The other decision variables depend on this.

Table 8.6: Decision Variables	
Variable Name	Variable Description
$NumStart_t$	Number of officers who start their shifts at time t
$NumPatrol_t$	Number of officers who are patrolling at time t
$Shortage_t$	Unmet demand at time t
$MaxShortage$	Maximum shortage across all times

Constraints

This use case imposes the following constraints:

$$\sum_t NumStart_t \leq capacity \tag{8.1}$$

$$NumPatrol_t = \sum_{s:t\in TIMES_s} NumStart_s \qquad \text{for all } t \tag{8.2}$$

$$Shortage_t \geq demand_t - NumPatrol_t \qquad \text{for all } t \tag{8.3}$$

$$MaxShortage \geq Shortage_t \qquad \text{for all } t \tag{8.4}$$

Constraint (8.1) enforces that at most the available number of officers are used. Constraint (8.2) defines the number of officers patrolling according to the number of officers who already started their shifts. Constraint (8.3) defines the shortage at time t. Constraint (8.4) defines the maximum shortage in terms of the shortage at time t.

Objective Functions

The primary objective in this use case is to minimize the total shortage:

$$\min \ TotalShortage = \sum_t Shortage_t$$

The secondary objective in this use case is to minimize the maximum shortage:

$$\min \ MaxShortage = \max_t Shortage_t$$

subject to an additional ("objective cut") constraint on total shortage (following the Sequential Algorithm mentioned in first section of this chapter)

$$TotalShortage \leq tolerance \times TotalShortage^* \qquad (8.5)$$

where $TotalShortage^*$ is the minimum total shortage.

8.2.4   Mathematical Formulation and SAS Model

Tables 8.7 and 8.8 show the mathematical formulation and the corresponding SAS code. Table 8.9 shows the SAS code for the sequential algorithm. The full code can be found in the supporting materials.

Table 8.7: SAS Code for Sets, Parameters, and Variables	
MATHEMATICS	**SAS CODE**
capacity	`num capacity = 40;`
duration	`num duration = 8;`
tolerance	`num tolerance = 1.1;`
$t \in \text{TIMES}$	`set TIMES;`
$demand_t$	`num demand {TIMES};`
maxTotalShortageBound	`num maxTotalShortageBound init 0;`
$NumStart_t$	`var NumStart {TIMES} >= 0 integer;`
$NumPatrol_t$	`var NumPatrol {TIMES} >= 0 integer;`
$Shortage_t$	`var Shortage {TIMES} >= 0 integer;`
MaxShortage	`var MaxShortage >= 0 integer;`

8.2 Use Case: Optimizing the Police Patrol Schedule

Table 8.8: SAS Code for Constraints and Objective Functions

$\sum_t NumStart_t \leq capacity$	```con CapacityCon:``` ``` sum {t in TIMES} NumStart[t] <= capacity;```

$NumPatrol_t = \sum_{s:t\in\text{TIMES}_s} NumStart_s$
for all t
	```con NumOfficersPatrollingCon {t in TIMES}:```
	``` NumPatrol[t] =```
	``` sum {s in TIMES: t in TIMES_shift[s]} NumStart[s];```

$Shortage_t \geq demand_t - NumPatrol_t$ for all t	```con ShortageCon {t in TIMES}:``` ``` Shortage[t] >= demand[t] - NumPatrol[t];```
$MaxShortage \geq Shortage_t$ for all t	```con MaxShortageCon {t in TIMES}:``` ``` MaxShortage >= Shortage[t];```
min $TotalShortage = \sum_t Shortage_t$	```impvar TotalShortage = sum {t in TIMES} Shortage[t];``` ```min MinTotalShortage = TotalShortage;```
min $MaxShortage$	```min MinMaxShortage = MaxShortage;```
$TotalShortage \leq$ $tolerance \times maxTotalShortageBound$	```con BoundCon:``` ``` TotalShortage <= tolerance * maxTotalShortageBound;```

Table 8.9: SAS Code for Sequential Optimization	
DESCRIPTION	SAS CODE
Run first solve	`solve obj MinTotalShortage;`
Record optimum TotalShortage to be used in Bound constraint	`maxTotalShortageBound = TotalShortage;`
Declare Bound constraint	`con BoundCon:` `  TotalShortage <= tolerance * maxTotalShortageBound;`
Run second solve	`solve obj MinMaxShortage;`

8.2.5   SAS Output

Figure 8.1 shows the Solution Summary produced by the SAS code after the first solve that minimizes Total Shortage. The optimum value for Total Shortage is 46, and the value for Maximum Shortage is 8. A more detailed sample output is presented in section 8.2.8.

Figure 8.2 shows the Solution Summary produced by the SAS code after the second solve that minimizes the Maximum Shortage, while not allowing the Total Shortage to go above the optimum value from the previous solve adjusted by a tolerance. After this solve, the optimum value for Maximum Shortage decreased from 8 to 3, and the value for Total Shortage increased from 46 to 50.

The SAS System

The OPTMODEL Procedure

Solution Summary	
Solver	MILP
Algorithm	Branch and Cut
Objective Function	MinTotalShortage
Solution Status	Optimal
Objective Value	46
Relative Gap	0
Absolute Gap	0
Primal Infeasibility	0
Bound Infeasibility	0
Integer Infeasibility	0
Best Bound	46
Nodes	1
Solutions Found	6
Iterations	39
Presolve Time	0.00
Solution Time	0.01

MinTotalShortage	MinMaxShortage
46	8

Figure 8.1: SAS Output

The SAS System

The OPTMODEL Procedure

Solution Summary	
Solver	MILP
Algorithm	Branch and Cut
Objective Function	MinMaxShortage
Solution Status	Optimal
Objective Value	3
Relative Gap	0
Absolute Gap	0
Primal Infeasibility	9.769963E-15
Bound Infeasibility	0
Integer Infeasibility	2.975398E-14
Best Bound	3
Nodes	1
Solutions Found	1
Iterations	55
Presolve Time	0.01
Solution Time	0.02

MinTotalShortage	MinMaxShortage
50	3

Figure 8.2: SAS Output

8.2.6   Mathematical Formulation and Python Model

Tables 8.10 and 8.11 show the mathematical formulation and the corresponding Python code. Table 8.12 shows the Python code for the sequential algorithm. The full code can be found in the supporting materials.

Table 8.10: Python Code for Sets, Parameters, and Variables	
MATHEMATICS	PYTHON CODE
capacity	`m.capacity = Param()`
duration	`m.duration = Param()`
tolerance	`m.tolerance = Param()`
$t \in$ TIMES	`m.times = Set()`
$demand_t$	`m.demand = Param(m.times)`
$maxTotalShortageBound$	`m.maxTotalShortageBound = Param(initialize=0, mutable=True)`
$NumStart_t$	`m.NumStart = Var(m.times, domain=NonNegativeIntegers)`
$NumPatrol_t$	`m.NumPatrol = Var(m.times, domain=NonNegativeIntegers)`
$Shortage_t$	`m.Shortage = Var(m.times, domain=NonNegativeIntegers)`
$MaxShortage$	`m.MaxShortage = Var(domain=NonNegativeIntegers)`

Table 8.11: Python Code for Constraints and Objective Functions

$\sum_t NumStart_t \leq capacity$	```def Capacity_Rule(m):
return (sum(m.NumStart[t] for t in m.times) <= m.capacity)
m.Capacity = Constraint(rule=Capacity_Rule)```
$NumPatrol_t = \sum_{s:t\in TIMES_s} NumStart_s$ for all t	```def Num_Patrol_Rule(m,t):
return (m.NumPatrol[t] ==
sum(m.NumStart[t1] for t1 in m.times if t-m.duration+1<=t1<=t) +
sum(m.NumStart[t1] for t1 in m.times if t1>=(max(m.times)-m.duration+2+t)))
m.Num_Patrol_Rule = Constraint(m.times,rule=Num_Patrol_Rule)```
$Shortage_t \geq demand_t - NumPatrol_t$ for all t	```def Define_Shortage_Rule(m,t):
return (m.Shortage[t] >= m.demand[t] - m.NumPatrol[t])
m.Define_Shortage = Constraint(m.times,rule=Define_Shortage_Rule)```
$MaxShortage \geq Shortage_t$ for all t	```def Define_Max_Shortage_Rule(m,t):
return (m.MaxShortage >= m.Shortage[t])
m.Define_Max_Shortage = Constraint(m.times,rule=Define_Max_Shortage_Rule)```
min $TotalShortage = \sum_t Shortage_t$	```def Min_Total_Shortage_Rule(m):
return sum(m.Shortage[t] for t in m.times)
m.Min_Total_Shortage = Objective(rule=Min_Total_Shortage_Rule, sense=minimize)```
min $MaxShortage$	```def Min_Max_Shortage_Rule(m):
return m.MaxShortage
m.Min_Max_Shortage = Objective(rule=Min_Max_Shortage_Rule, sense=minimize)```
$TotalShortage \leq$ $tolerance \times maxTotalShortageBound$	```def Bound_Rule(m):
return (m.Min_Total_Shortage <= m.tolerance*m.maxTotalShortageBound)
m.Bound = Constraint(rule=Bound_Rule)```

Table 8.12: Python Code for Sequential Optimization	
DESCRIPTION	PYTHON CODE (To be run after building instance data)
Deactivate Bound constraint and Min_Max_Shortage objective	`m.Bound.deactivate()` `m.Min_Max_Shortage.deactivate()`
Create instance	`instance = m.create_instance(InstanceData)`
Choose solver and run first solve	`solver = SolverFactory("glpk")` `solution=solver.solve(instance)`
Use optimum TotalShortage in Bound constraint and activate constraint	`maxTotalShortageBound=value(instance.TotalShortage)` `m.Bound.activate()`
Deactivate Min_Total_Shortage and activate Min_Max_Shortage objectives	`m.Min_Total_Shortage.deactivate()` `m.Min_Max_Shortage.activate()`
Create instance	`instance = m.create_instance(InstanceData)`
Choose solver and run second solve	`solver = SolverFactory("glpk")` `solution=solver.solve(instance)`

8.2.7   Python Output

Figure 8.3 shows the output produced by the Python code after the first solve that minimizes Total Shortage. The optimum value for Total Shortage is 46, and the value for Maximum Shortage is 7. A more detailed sample output is presented in section 8.2.8.

Figure 8.4 shows the output produced by the Python code after the second solve that minimizes the Maximum Shortage, while not allowing the Total Shortage to go above the optimum value from the previous solve adjusted by a tolerance. After this solve, the optimum value for Maximum Shortage decreased from 7 to 3, and the value for Total Shortage increased from 46 to 47.

```
- Status: ok
  Termination condition: optimal
  Statistics:
    Branch and bound:
      Number of bounded subproblems: 1
      Number of created subproblems: 1
  Error rc: 0
  Time: 0.042832136154174805

Optimum Total Shortage Value:
46.0
Max Shortage Value:
7.0
```

Figure 8.3: Python Output

```
- Status: ok
  Termination condition: optimal
  Statistics:
    Branch and bound:
      Number of bounded subproblems: 1
      Number of created subproblems: 1
  Error rc: 0
  Time: 0.04799842834472656

Optimum Max Shortage Value:
3.0
Total Shortage Value:
47.0
```

Figure 8.4: Python Output

8.2.8 Output Results

Table 8.13 shows a snapshot of an optimal number of officers who should start
their shifts at each hour. Figure 8.5 shows a plot of an optimal solution for the
primary objective of minimizing the total shortage. Figure 8.6 shows a plot of
an optimal solution for the secondary objective of minimizing the maximum
shortage.

Table 8.13: Optimal Results Data Snapshot

Time	NumStart
15	4
16	9
17	0

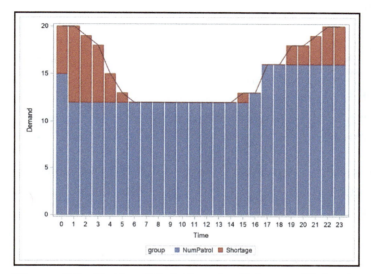

Figure 8.5: Optimal Solution for Primary Objective

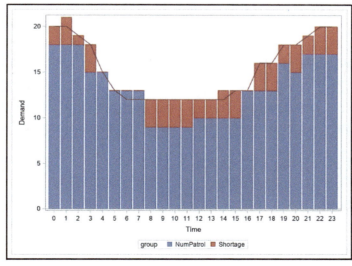

Figure 8.6: Optimal Solution for Secondary Objective

8.3   Practice Problems

1. The North Carolina Tourism State Agency is required to coordinate all efforts to attract tourism industry to the state. The agency received five proposals for projects, such as destinations marketing and infrastructure improvements, and must attempt to schedule these projects in the following two weeks. Assume that each project duration is one week and each project can be launched in only one of the two weeks. Each project's cost depends on which week the project is going to be scheduled and is provided in the MC_P1_project_costs.csv data. In addition, projects with IDs 2 and 5 cannot be scheduled together in the same week, each project can be scheduled only once, and not every project has to be scheduled. The agency has a total budget of $100,000 for the entire planning period.

   Pro Bono Analytics volunteers came up with a regression-based model that estimates the impact of these projects in tourism affluence (in number of tourists) as well as expenditure per tourist (in dollars). This information is provided in the MC_P2_project_master.csv data.

   (a) Find the project scheduling solution that maximizes the total expenditure (total dollars all visiting tourists will spend).
   (b) Find the project scheduling solution that maximizes the total number of visitors (tourists).
   (c) Assume that priority one for the agency is to maximize the total expenditure. However, they also want to maximize number of tourists as priority two while guaranteeing that total expenditure is within 10% of the optimum value.

2. For the police patrol schedule use case, use the MOD function to rewrite the index set for the sum in the NumOfficersPatrollingCon constraint as follows.
   ```
   set TIMES_shift {s in TIMES} =
   setof {t in s..s+duration-1} mod(t,maxTime+1);
   ```

3. For the police patrol schedule use case, use the LINEARIZE option in SAS to automatically linearize the MAX operator as follows. Omit the Shortage and MaxShortage variables, omit the ShortageCon and MaxShortageCon

constraints, declare Shortage as an implicit variable, and declare the two
objectives:

```
impvar Shortage {t in TIMES} =
 max(demand[t] - NumPatrol[t], 0);
min MinTotalShortage = sum {t in TIMES} Shortage[t];
min MinMaxShortage = max {t in TIMES} Shortage[t];
```

Then use the LINEARIZE option in each solve statement. For example,
the first one becomes:

```
solve obj MinTotalShortage linearize;
```

Chapter 9

Practice Problem Solutions

9.1 Linear Programming (Chapter 4)

Problem 1: Hire 10 in years 1 and 2 and let go 20 in year 3.

9.2 Mixed Integer Linear Programming (Chapter 5)

Problem 1: Select beams 1 and 3.

Problem 2.a: Schedule 3 spots in show 1/day 2, 2 spots in show 2/day 2, 1 spot in show 3/day 2, and 3 spots in show 4/day 2.

Problem 2.b: 50 million.

Problem 2.c: $250,000.

9.3 Nonlinear Optimization (Chapter 6)

Problem 1: Optimum revenue (accounting for disposal costs) is $518.86.

9.4   Network Optimization (Chapter 7)

Problem 1: Assign CT to region 1, NJ to region 2, and PA to region 3.

9.5   Multicriteria Optimization (Chapter 8)

Problem 1.a: Schedule project 2 in week 2 and project 3 in week 2.

Problem 1.b: Schedule project 1 in week 1, project 5 in week 1, project 3 in week 2, and project 4 in week 2.

Problem 1.c: Schedule project 2 in week 2 and project 4 in week 2.

Bibliography

[ABCC06]   D.L. Applegate, R.E. Bixby, V. Chvátal, and W.J. Cook. *The Traveling Salesman Problem: A Computational Study.* Princeton, NJ: Princeton University Press, 2006.

[Alb20]   Keith Albertson. Students help mothers' milk bank expand its reach, save expenses. `https://www.iise.org/iemagazine/2020-01/html/case-study/case-study.html`, 2020.

[Ber91]   Dimitri P. Bertsekas. *Linear Network Optimization: Algorithms and Codes.* MIT Press, 1991.

[BFG+01]   Kenneth P. Botwin, Eric D. Freeman, Robert D. Gruber, et al. Radiation exposure to the physician performing fluoroscopically guided caudal epidural steroid injections. *Pain Physician*, 4(4):343–348, 2001.

[BHH+21]   Michael L. Bynum, Gabriel A. Hackebeil, William E. Hart, et al. *Pyomo—Optimization Modeling in Python.* Cham, Switzerland: Springer Science & Business Media, Third edition, 2021.

[BHRE12]   Ruud Brekelmans, Dick den Hertog, Kees Roos, and Carel Eijgenraam. Safe dike heights at minimal costs: The nonhomogeneous case. *Operations Research*, 60(6):1342–1355, 2012.

[BSS13]   Mokhtar S. Bazaraa, Hanif D. Sherali, and Chitharanjan M. Shetty. *Nonlinear Programming: Theory and Algorithms.* John Wiley & Sons, 2013.

[BT97]   Dimitris Bertsimas and John N. Tsitsiklis. *Introduction to Linear Optimization*, volume 6. Belmont, MA: Athena Scientific, 1997.

[BW05]   Dimitris Bertsimas and Robert Weismantel. *Optimization over Integers*, volume 13. Dynamic Ideas, 2005.

[dt12]   The GLPK development team. GLPK (GNU Linear Programming Kit). `https://www.gnu.org/software/glpk/`, 2012.

[dt20]   The pandas development team. pandas-dev/pandas: Pandas, February 2020.

[dt22a]   The IPOPT development team. IPOPT. `https://coin-or.github.io/Ipopt/`, 2022.

[dt22b]   The Jupyter development team. Jupyter Notebook 6.4.12. https://jupyter.org/, 2022.

[dt22c]   The NumPy development team. NumPy 1.23.3. https://numpy.org/, 2022.

[dt22d]   The pandas development team. Pandas 1.4.3. https://pandas.pydata.org/, 2022.

[dt22e]   The Pyomo development team. Pyomo 6.4.2. http://www.pyomo.org/, 2022.

[dt22f]   The Python development team. Python 3.10.4. https://www.python.org/downloads/release/python-3104/, 2022.

[EBdHR17]   Carel Eijgenraam, Ruud Brekelmans, Dick den Hertog, and Kees Roos. Optimal strategies for flood prevention. *Management Science*, 63(5):1644–1656, 2017.

[Ehr05]   Matthias Ehrgott. *Multicriteria Optimization*, volume 491. Springer Science & Business Media, 2005.

[GDJ+23]   Emma Gibson, Sarang Deo, Jónas Oddur Jónasson, et al. Redesigning sample transportation in Malawi through improved data sharing and daily route optimization. *Manufacturing & Service Operations Management*, 25(4):1209–1226, 2023.

[HMvdW+20] Charles R. Harris, K. Jarrod Millman, Stéfan J. van der Walt, et al. Array programming with NumPy. *Nature*, 585(7825):357–362, September 2020.

[HWW11]   William E. Hart, Jean-Paul Watson, and David L. Woodruff. Pyomo: modeling and solving mathematical programs in Python. *Mathematical Programming Computation*, 3(3):219–260, 2011.

[Las19]   Rob Lasson. From donors to babies. `https://www.ise.ncsu.edu/blog/2019/10/23/from-donors-to-babies/`, 2019.

[LD60]   Ailsa H. Land and Alison G. Doig. An automatic method of solving discrete programming problems. *Econometrica: Journal of the Econometric Society*, 28(3):497–520, 1960.

[LZ08]   Eva K. Lee and Marco Zaider. Operations research advances cancer therapeutics. *Interfaces*, 38(1):5–25, 2008.

[MTZ60]   C.E. Miller, A.W. Tucker, and R.A. Zemlin. Integer programming formulation of traveling salesman problems. *Journal of the Association for Computing Machinery*, 7:326–329, 1960.

[Paz20]   Subramanian Pazhani. Back to school optimization. `https://blogs.sas.com/content/operations/2020/10/26/backtoschooloptimization/`, 2020.

[PSG+21]   Koen Peters, Sérgio Silva, Rui Goncalves, et al. The nutritious supply chain: optimizing humanitarian food assistance. *INFORMS Journal on Optimization*, 3(2):200–226, 2021.

[SAS23]   SAS Institute Inc. SAS Optimization: Mathematical Optimization Procedures. `https://go.documentation.sas.com/doc/en/pgmsascdc/v_042/casmopt/titlepage.htm`, 2023.

[Sum20] Natalia Summerville. Mathematical Optimization to Support Safe Back-to-School. `https://www.linkedin.com/pulse/mathematical-optimization-support-safe-back-to-school-summerville`, 2020.

[TH89] Philip E. Taylor and Stephen J. Huxley. A break from tradition for the San Francisco police: Patrol officer scheduling using an optimization-based decision support system. *INFORMS Journal on Applied Analytics*, 19(1):4–24, 1989.

[WB06] Andreas Wächter and Lorenz T. Biegler. On the implementation of an interior-point filter line-search algorithm for large-scale nonlinear programming. *Mathematical Programming*, 106(1):25–57, 2006.

[WM10] Wes McKinney. Data Structures for Statistical Computing in Python. In Stéfan van der Walt and Jarrod Millman, editors, *Proceedings of the 9th Python in Science Conference*, pages 56–61, 2010.

[Wol20] Laurence A. Wolsey. *Integer Programming*. John Wiley & Sons, 2020.

[ZHZ+22] Masoud Zarepisheh, Linda Hong, Ying Zhou, et al. Automated and clinically optimal treatment planning for cancer radiotherapy. *INFORMS Journal on Applied Analytics*, 52(1):69–89, 2022.

www.ingramcontent.com/pod-product-compliance
Lightning Source LLC
LaVergne TN
LVHW080117070326
832902LV00015B/2635

9 781955 977838